AIR WAR DIARY

AIR WAR DIARY

DAVID SCHOLES, D.F.C.

Kangaroo Press

DEDICATED TO MY WIFE, PAT
THE DIARY'S INSPIRATION

ALSO BY DAVID SCHOLES

Fly Fisher in Tasmania
The Way of an Angler
Trout Quest
Tasmanian Angler
Fly Fishing in Australia
Trutta the Trout
Trout Days
Ripples, Runs and Rises
Fly Fishing Pictorial (with Tony Ritchie)
Trout and Trouting

COVER: Bombing up N-Nan — a record of 100 Ops before collapse.
FRONTISPIECE: Lancasters of 61 Squadron set out on a daylight raid.

First published in 1997 by Kangaroo Press Pty Ltd
3 Whitehall Road, Kenthurst NSW 2156 Australia
P.O. Box 6125 Dural Delivery Centre NSW 2158
Printed by Australian Print Group, Maryborough 3465

ISBN 0 86417 837 9

PREFACE

Because the events I propose retelling took place some fifty years ago, I realise that for many of my readers I am speaking of an entirely different period, before television, for example, and such commonplace things as supermarkets and motels. I am concerned with history, a time of war, world war; confined to that part of it which occurred in the air — in my case aerial bombardment in Europe — a subject strange to many readers even of my own age. Moreover, the places where these things happened have in some cases changed considerably. Cities and towns that were burnt to the ground and reduced to rubble have been rebuilt. Others expanded and new ones have been created. The landscape has altered, new roads and railways now line the maps and virgin forest has become agricultural land.

Yet, in spite of all this change, I have been so urged by people, both young and old, to tell my story that I am convinced there is genuine interest. But I do not intend producing another narrative war book. There have been many of these, some superbly written and illustrated, covering all three services, and I warmly commend them.

I kept a diary from the day I left Australia until the day I returned. This, plus a wealth of illustrative material which I accumulated, allows me to provide an accurate account of what took place when and where. For anyone requiring a detailed and complete record of Bomber Command's history and operations I refer you to *Bomber Offensive* by Marshal of the RAF Sir Arthur Harris. In my memory there are numerous events that might have been included in my story, but they cannot be added now. It would be akin to working over an old painting, adding touches that you think would improve it, but destroying the originality of the work and its authenticity.

This journal was written in some detail and records events, sights and actions seen through the eyes of a twenty-year-old war pilot using the words he spoke then to describe his thoughts at that moment and also what he saw. A fifty year old wartime diary will inevitably include some words that would cause offence if used so casually today. I regret this, but readers putting themselves in my position at the time will, I believe, understand.

The diary divides rather well into five parts — I hope readers will find that this structure provides suitable breaks in the narrative. It begins with a preamble written by Kathleen Partridge in her little book, *Through Life's Lattice,* and to create the right setting of what follows I quote it now:

> I hope I shall be present at that future day of days when a noble world rebuilds upon the ruins of the past. I seek no fierce excitement and no firework displays, but a plan of great perfection — an improvement on the last.
>
> Where poverty unknown is and the joys of life increase. Where bright and airy thoroughfares replace a darkened slum. Where the milk of human kindness is a better phrase for peace, and security is commonplace and evil overcome.
>
> Where old folk need not tremble nor the young fear being slain. Where finer dwellings rise upon the narrow sites of old. Where people who have parted have their loved ones back again. Thus good shall spring from evil, as the prophets have foretold.
>
> When everyone is filled with the desire to be good friends. When nobody begrudges what another person spends. When people are contented with the things they can afford, and help each other for the sake of goodwill not reward.
>
> When roses rank with rubies for their beauty not their worth, and folk find joy in sharing all the loveliness on earth. Then and only then will greed and hostile aims decrease. A world that holds enough for all will know the joys of peace.

To relate the entire day-by-day record of my overseas service would become tiresome and at times repetitive. Instead I have deleted entries which are unimportant or irrelevant. This aids continuity. The diary contains a number of abbreviations, a glossary of which is listed at the book's end. To use their full titles in the text would often result in the loss of characteristic wartime airforce jargon and sometimes the precise circumstances surrounding a particular entry.

Of the 250 000 aircrew who operated within Bomber Command, 44 000 were killed in action, the sentiments of Sir Arthur Harris summarising the particulars both clearly and proudly: 'There are no words with which I can do justice to the aircrew who fought under my command. There is no parallel in warfare to such courage and determination in the face of danger over so prolonged a period, of danger which at times was so great that scarcely one man in three could expect to survive his tour of thirty operations.'

David Scholes
Launceston, 1996

CONTENTS

ENGLAND; SHOWING CITIES, TOWNS AND BASES MENTIONED IN TEXT

PART 1

TO AMERICA

Wednesday 26 May 1943 (1 pm): We leave Sydney Harbour — more than that we leave Australia! The bridge looks greater and more magnificent than ever before. We have an Australian destroyer with us. What for? Don't we all know. A few of us stand at the stern of the ship. I take in everything I see. We pass out through the Heads, the destroyer out ahead. We all seem very silent now, except for an odd wisecrack. I suppose everyone is thinking more or less the same as I am. There is that faint haunting feeling now, 'I wonder — yes, of course we will'. But I still wonder. We are still silent, and Australia slowly grows smaller, rapidly comes more dear to me. It disappears below the green watery horizon. 'There she goes fellas'!

Saturday 29 May: About 1 pm I see my first glimpses of New Zealand. Until 8 pm we sail down the east coast, finally berthing at Auckland in the dark. I go to bed about 10.45 pm.

Sunday 30 May: Manage to wangle our way off the ship and see a little of Auckland. Unfortunately it is Sunday and we cannot buy anything — perhaps just as well for I am almost flat broke now! I write a brief note home from Hotel Auckland, and also one to Pat. I find Auckland quite an amazing place, but the flaming Yanks have spoilt it quite a bit already no doubt. I fill up with steak, eggs and tomatoes for I am sure I won't see any for some time — even if I could eat them. The view from the extinct volcano, Mt Eden, is wonderful. After tea several of us toddle along to a dance at the Town Hall. I shall always remember the three Maoris who sang, 'The Maori's Farewell'.

Monday 31 May: We leave Auckland. A Harvard makes a poor attempt at a shoot up. I stand on deck in the sun and watch the little islands slip by as we weave our way out. All day, until dusk, we are escorted by Hudsons of RNZAF. At length the last one dives past us as a salute and heads away behind us just as the huge red sun vanishes behind the dark, may I even say sinister horizon. We are alone now. Look out America, here we come.

Wednesday 2 June: Today we cross the International Date Line and we put our watches back 24 hours, so we have another Monday! Not feeling exactly like a game of football, but have not been over the side yet.

Thursday 3 June: Can now almost propel myself in the desired direction in nearly a straight line, perhaps I am gaining my 'sea legs'! I do not eat much, in any case the 'chow' as the Yanks, who run this apology for a ship, call it is not exactly like Australian food. When it comes to putting jam on bacon and syrup on meats etc, things are a little strange in my opinion. I live by stealing sufficient grapefruit, oranges, apples, biscuits and dry food, and buying at the ship's canteen drinks such as Coca Cola and Pepsi Cola. Have no idea where we are as we steer a course varying between 000° and about 160°, however we're still floating.

Saturday 5 June: I have been issued with a comforts fund parcel, in which I find all sorts of stuff — mittens, writing material, sheep skin jacket, socks, scarf, sea water soap, sweater, tooth paste and numerous other things —all the more to carry!

Sunday 6 June: At 38 minutes past nine am we cross the Equator and it is extremely hot, although out on deck it is nice and cool with the breeze. We flop about the deck sunbathing and sleeping. The officers go through the 'Neptune' ceremony, a tradition of the Navy, in the form of an initiation. The crew are all togged up in hideous rig-outs for the occasion, and go to town on the boys in no uncertain fashion.

I find the flying fish quite fascinating flitting about the surface of the sea in odd ones and twos, and sometimes in great numbers. The sea has been quite calm lately and is very blue, bluer than anything imaginable. One of our sprog P/Os is making himself extremely unpopular amongst the boys. (P/O Jones.) I wonder can he swim! In any case it's a long swim to the nearest land if he does slip overboard.

Wednesday 9 June: Have been writing a considerable number of letters home and to Pat, also writing a note or two to all sorts of people whom I have met at different times and have their address.

As we find our quarters a bit warm for sleeping we carry all our junk up on deck and camp the night there. I find it wonderful to go to sleep 'under the stars', until (usually about 2.30 am) rain becomes evident.

Friday 11 June: Today we are picked up and escorted by aircraft and a Navy Blimp. It is quite foggy and we cannot see the Golden Gate of San Francisco until we are almost under it. Sure is a noble lump of engineering, but I am not as struck with it as I thought I would be — most amusing the 'Golden Gate' being painted a dirty red. Past the bridge on the left is Golden Gate Park, and behind that very beautiful mountains and hill country. We pass very close by the island-prison of Alcatraz. We are advised by the Yanks, who jibber now like niggers, (I have taken a distinct dislike to them on the whole) that only one man has ever escaped from here. Treasure Island, famous because the New York World Fair was held there, is also visible. At length we dock and we are greatly disappointed because we cannot leave the ship — seeing land again after some time at sea is really something to me now.

We gaze at 'Frisco' until it is dark and turn in — what a hell of a long way I am from home!

Saturday 12 June: We disembark from U.S.S. 'MOUNT VERNON' — as might be expected (before war U.S.S. 'WASHINGTON') there is quite a lump of panic. Here we are decidedly up in arms against the Yanks, for that part of our baggage that was put in the hold had been ripped open and anything of value at all, especially cameras, new shoes and clothes etc., has been taken. It is too late to do anything about it.

We board a ferry and go to Oatlands across the harbour. There are numerous submarines, destroyers, cruisers, aircraft carriers and all types of naval craft about. One carrier is loaded with Lockheed Lightnings. Formations of Avengers, Martletts, Airacobras, Lightnings, Mitchells, Bostons, Liberators, Mariners, Catalinas, Marauders, and all types of aircraft are numerous. Across at Oatlands we get into a Pullman DeLuxe railroad service train. At 1300 we leave Oatlands and San Francisco. The boys are very taken with the appearance at least, of American girls!

We pass through Albamount, Quisley and Stockton. Soon we pass a training airfield equipped with Steerman or Boeing trainers. The land here in California is quite like some parts of New South Wales. I am enjoying this very much. We have plenty of room and a berth each. When I think of all the land that we have yet to cross, I reckon this is 'just the shot!' Late in the afternoon we pull up at Sacramento, a truly beautiful little town with huge elms and plane trees on each side of the avenues. The homes have no fences, neither outside nor dividing them. Every home has a huge shining modern car. The houses are all wooden with tin roofs. I like this little town in California very much, but still do not like Yanks!

Just before dusk we pass through the pleasant, busy town of Marysville, the name reminding me of home (Victoria).

Sunday 13 June: We have crossed the Sierra Nevadas during the night and have missed seeing them — poor show! We are out of California and into Nevada now. We pass through Gulacki, Jungo and Pronto. The railway follows the plains, which stretch for miles covered with salt bush. In the distance there are very rugged mountains, some covered with snow. There is a distinct beauty about this country although it is not very colourful. We get out for a 'stretch' at Winnemucca, and I take a couple of photographs — I wish I had more film for there is plenty worth photographing.

Our next stops are Battle Mountains, Dunphy, Elko and Wendover, the latter on the border of Nevada and Utah. It is both an airport and air Army Centre, and I dangle out of windows to yarn to a bunch of Yank airmen and find that they bite very well!

Off again and we pass through mile after mile of salt plains before reaching Salt Lake City, late in the afternoon. It is a considerable size and already the neon lights are blazing. It seems to be spread out over a great amount of land, which of course is very flat.

Evening comes on as we leave.

Monday 14 June: We wake to find ourselves in the state of Colorado. Before we have quite finished breakfast (meals being brought to us on cardboard plates, cardboard spoons, forks and cups also being provided, and the meals a great deal better, both in quality and also I suppose in the fact that we feel more like eating now. Actually I am always hungry! About twice a day candy is brought also) we pass Glenwood. Here we begin to climb the famous Rocky Mountains. The line follows the Leadsville Gorge, in which flows the swift Colorado River, all the way up. The line twists and turns, sometimes crossing the river, the train whistle echoes and re-echoes amongst the towering cliffs and crags. The air becomes more crisp as we climb. The foliage becomes dense and shines with its dampness. There are pines, silver birches, maples and fir trees, there are many types of grasses and wild flowers, pink, yellow, blue and cream. The river is but a stream now, clear and cold, and runs over a bed of stone and rocks which in some spots turn it into a foaming rush. We are amongst patches of snow now. I find a couple of chaps fly fishing in the stream, one has a fine steelhead trout hanging from his side — I turn a vivid green with envy! This scenery is amazing. I shall never forget it.

At the summit it is cold. There are snow-capped peaks all around us and the pines all covered and drooping with snow, seem to be about the only trees able to stand up to these conditions. The line picks up the Arkansas River and we begin to follow this down the other side of the Rockies.

I write home and to Pat. It is good to think of everything back in Australia. We get talking now and then about it.

This side of the Rockies is much the same, but a little more on the dry and rugged side, especially as we get lower down. Soon after dinner we get out for a while at Salida, the whole place reminding me at once of the 'America' I have seen so often on the screen. The water in the Arkansas is quite brown here and the stream must be about 40 yards in width. There are numerous small willows along the banks. All the towns in this state have the first letter of the name prominently displayed on the side of a nearby mountain to aid air navigation. Here we have a huge white 'S' standing well out.

We go on down through the world famous Royal Gorge, a long narrow canyon of immense depth, at some parts it is quite a thousand feet. The railroad here is the world's steepest in incline. High above us at one point is the world's highest single span suspension bridge across the gorge, 1053 feet above the Arkansas below. It is very hot now down at the bottom of the canyon, for there is no breeze and the sun streams straight down. I am down to the bare minimum of shorts and shoes — some are below minimum! We were all shivering a while ago. We run out of the gorge into a surprising green valley and here we find the little settlement of Canyon City. The flats of the Arkansas are well used here, every yard ploughed or in crop. There are huge green elms and high green grass all around. It becomes cooler so on go the clothes again!

The next large town is Pueblo, from what we can gather 'a dangerous joint'. There are quite a lot of evil looking bodies about, the females equally evil looking as the men! Here our black porter Joe, Shady, Moonlight, or whatever we call him, misses the train whilst getting the boys some candy and postcards. However he picks us up again at a crossing just out of town, having taken a taxi. He is all smiles of triumph as he regains the train. (I can see Pike's Peak — 14,050 ft covered with snow and standing right out.)

We have packs of American cigarettes given to us each day — anyone would think we didn't have enough! I have been smoking nothing but these, such as Chesterfield, Old Gold, Lucky Strike, Philip Morris, Pall Mall etc. ever since we were 500 miles from Australia.

The outskirts of the place seem just as wicked, rampant with crime. We must have missed those Pueblo Indians. 'Back again after the war' — like all the journey so far. We are on the Santa Fe Trail now with a huge Santa Fe R.R. loco pulling us at some 70 to 90 mph. Still in the state of Colorado. Rocky Ford and La Junta slide past. Syracuse, the oft-mentioned town on the screen, seems quite a large place. About midnight we stop for a short time at the well-known Dodge City — cannot see much of the place. It is a blaze of lights — in the state of Kansas now — into bed, a weed and off to sleep.

Tuesday 15 June: 'Good mo'nin suh. Ah kin put up yo' bed whenever yo' like.' I blink at the coloured porter muttering, 'Wha? Oh, yes, thanks mate.'

On through the fertile black soil plains of Kansas, (for we have crossed the Colorado-Kansas border during the night.) There are growing crops of corn and other grasses, with typical white wooden houses, plenty of shaded streets and well-tilled earth, past Emporia. I like the American habit of planting trees wherever possible. In combination with the absence of fences and lawns out to the edge of the street it gives an atmosphere of coolness and dignity. Going out of Emporia the train passes through a pleasant park of cut grass and green trees, with the name of the town in concrete.

Maize seems the best grower here in the Kansas plains, where it is good the oats and wheat is spindly, short in the stem, poor in the ear as might be expected. There are frequent blue and yellow wildflowers a little like larkspurs, and white ones a bit like poppies, and some others. It seems that Kansas is one of the few remaining prohibition states. The other two are Oklahoma and Mississippi. The matter is of more than academic interest to us. Now through the glorious woods of light green trees — elms and poplars. Suddenly the Missouri River comes alongside, about a hundred yards wide, brown and swollen. Across another state border we go into Missouri. At length we roll into Kansas City, the heart of this huge industrial centre, surrounded by huge grain silos, manufacturing plants, railroad activity, typical mid-west white wooden houses, mostly fenceless, with green roofs.

Out we go along the Altona R.R., through hamlets at close intervals in fertile, attractive close farming country — Odessa, Marshall, Norton and Slater, where we get out and buy food and Coca Cola. We continue through similar farm lands, through Centralia and Mexico. I see a few Hereford steers and Ryeland — (I think) sheep about.

An oak wood of thousands of acres, full of attractive possibilities, precedes Louisiana. We cross the wide Mississippi River swollen in flood and a chocolate brown colour for they have had abnormal rains here lately. Old Man River has overflowed in parts and spreads for hundreds of acres — our porter tells us 'he's a wicked ole river'. The levies are apparently not very effective when a real flood comes down. Having crossed the river we are now in Illinois. At Roadhouse the Victory gardens look well in the rich black earth. We stop soon at the large, clean, bright city of Springfield. I hang out the window with some postcards and photo — books of Royal Gorge and ask a wizard of a skirt to post them. She seems amused at our speech (the feeling is mutual). She flatly refuses to take the money. Dusk is gathering now as we move on. We are all waiting eagerly to see Chicago. Life in the train has been quite good considering. We play cards and there always seems plenty of fun about, and plenty to look at. At Joliet there are huge petrol and oil storage facilities.

At length at about 2230 we reach Chicago a huge city as it appears, brightly lit with a mist from Lake Michigan hanging over it. The population I am told is some three to four million. Chicago, I have always believed, is the home of gangsterism. I expect at any minute to see Edward G. Robinson or Humphrey Bogart come toddling up the line, or in through the window. We get out of the train and walk about the railroad tracks nearly getting skittled by huge fast electric trains, streamlined to perfection and glittering in the brightly lit night. We change to a diesel engine, and at about 5 past one in the morning leave Chicago, and soon get up to a steady 80 to 90 mph.

I go to bed at 0146 hours.

Wednesday 16 June: I waken in the state of Indiana, where the farming lands, well grassed, range from black to fawn. I have had enough black, for cinders up to an eighth of an inch in diameter have been coming into the carriage from this flaming engine. What I want is a decent shower, a bucket of beer, and a bed that keeps still. I shall arrive at the East Coast looking as though I had flown through the Battle of Britain, and not changed since! We stop at Fort Wayne where a Yank inquires where we are from 'AUSTRALIA'! reply the boys. 'Where's that, Missouri?' he asks — wouldn't it! We have been in Indiana for some time and here we slip across the border into Ohio and pass through similar farming country with many villages and towns — making good time now, someone claims to have clocked us at 96 mph. I time it twice getting an average of 78.

Some excellent wheat crops for grain here in Ohio. At Crestline we halt for a stretch, then off again through Mansfield and Massillon, where heavy metal industries are springing up — Canton too is similar. The sun is hot, although the sky is overcast. A blue haze dims the distant trees. Pass through Alliance and Salem — poor dumps on the whole, and across the Ohio-Pennsylvania border. Beaver Hills and Rochester are manufacturing towns of some size. The people here must take more pride in their homes than those of Ohio and Illinois. They use paints of different colour, and paint more often! Past Rochester flows the Ohio River — a fairly broad stream and there is an old steel smelting works on the far bank from us. Vessels of perhaps 300 to 400 tons pass up and down the stream. Here we become homesick for there is a perfect small scale Sydney Harbour bridge spanning the river.

During the trip I have seen numerous strange birds which I cannot identify. Some are very pretty, others have a peculiar flight. I am fascinated by the little, furry grey 'Gophers'. They are about the size of a big squirrel, also having a squirrel-like tail. They live underground and sit outside their holes full of curiosity and mischief as we pass. When frightened or disturbed, they can run like hell. They are quite harmless and do no damage. On from Pittsburg after a short wait, through extensive suburbs to the south, some of them not attractive, and plunge into the Alleghenies where we meet a stream. We pass a mineral recovering dredge and a remarkable locomotive dragging track-sweeping apparatus.

Buy 'Altoona Mirror' (circulation 29,000) and some Pepsi Cola from a small nigger. We reach Harrisburg, a large city — capital I think of Pennsylvania. Here we change to an electric loco which will take us on the run through Philadelphia to, and under New York. Harrisburg is much cleaner than Pittsburg — didn't like the latter at all. Just the same, I cannot see much of it. This Pennsylvania RR is immense with track, locos and rolling stock. After leaving Harrisburg I am amazed at the speed at which this electric loco pulls us along — the mechanical stoker on the steam loco we had from Pittsburg gave us all the screamers, and we find this type of engine far better from a passenger's point of view. (The mechanical stoker on the steam loco crushes the coal into large powder form and hurls it into the furnace, where it burns with a gaseous flame. The resultant clinker flies back along and into the train, we were all covered with it, even though our windows were closed. (It seems the Pennsylvania R.R. is making a great number of people black to save one or two from it!)

Before dark we arrive at Philadelphia which I like very much. It is a pretty city with plenty of trees and open park land. The roads all appear to be of white concrete, and here we get our first idea of American traffic. The cars are all extremely modern. There seems not to be a car more than four years old on the roads. Into the state of New Jersey and we come to New Brunswick and Newark. It is almost dusk now and we are keen to reach New York before dark.

At 2004 hours we enter the huge subway passing under New York and under the Hudson River. We miss most of the city but when we come out at the other end we can see some huge skyscrapers and buildings in the distance. We have been told that we shall have the chance to see it, so we are not too wild about it. At 10 o'clock we are at Newhaven, and soon after midnight we make our final halt at an army siding near Taunton in Massachusetts. We are all a bit weary and are not too proud to go straight to bed in very decent quarters.

Thursday 17 June: This is Camp Miles Standish. It is an embarkation depot for American forces, and there are thousands of them about — I can see we shall be happy. I believe Providence and Boston are not far away. I find the canteens — 'post exchanges' as they call them here, truly marvellous. There is everything inside imaginable — miniature Myer Emporiums! First we taste the beer, which isn't too bad! We eat enough candy ice-cream and chocolate to sink a ship. I have not half explored the camp yet. It is immense. I have found three huge dance halls, four picture theatres and ten canteens so far. I am very amazed. I think we all are. I cable home and Pat — $6.05 ie 38/- each!

We cannot leave camp this first night but still a lot of us do, by Aussie tactics dazzle the Yank guards with science and toddle down the road to Wiltown, a small village where we spend more money on some of these amazing American dishes and drinks I still do not know the name of yet. We get into conversation with men, women and children. So this is America from outside the train window!

Friday 18 June: I begin the day after breakfast by writing home to Pat and 'Snake'. Continue to have a marvellous time — am very fit, well and happy, there is always something new to do and see. We are given three and a half days leave to New York. (The gunners are going to Boston.) I have decided to buy Pat a wrist watch and see a good looking Hamilton in one of the PXs for $65.00, but it is not good enough.

Am going into Taunton tonight on the bash.

Saturday 19 June: We set off for New York and are driven to Providence by buses, and here we catch a fast electric train which will take us to New York City in four hours. From the station Wal Summerton, Stan Silver, George Surgeoner and myself taxi to the Anzac Club where we get the GO on the best places to stay and what to do and see. We stay at an Overseas Legion turn out which we find very pleasant.

It is late afternoon so we cannot go far afield, and at length after a cold shower, for it is very humid and hot, (and we are <u>not</u> allowed to wear our shorts in this country outside camp!) Wal and I taxi to the USO Club in East 68th Street, which is an immense place for forces. There we have tea which I think is the best meal I have had since we left Australia. There is a huge dance floor, a roof garden (only 29 floors above), ping pong gear, pianos, writing facilities and all manner of amusements. We stay a short time and after visiting the roof garden where we meet 'R-Rita', best forgotten, Wal and I set off for Times Square, Broadway — the playground of a nation.

It is Saturday night on Broadway in New York and they don't mean maybe. I shall never forget the crowds on Broadway and 42nd Street. We poke about here and there aiming to see as much as possible. I am amazed with the interior of the Waldorf Astoria, one of New York's largest Hotel De Luxes, and reputed to be the most beautiful. The tall highly polished columns of marble surrounding the inner hall, the blue glass steps on either side up to a circular lounge, the large colourful designs on the walls, the glittering chandeliers and living greeneries take your breath away. We visit the Oasis Room, one of the many little private drinking rooms with various names and have a Tom Collins and a Zombie each for $5.80.

Back to Broadway and into a circus for a while, and it is a circus. Here we met a Yank Navigator who takes us to the Hurricane Club where we see Duke Ellington and his famous Band in action and have a drink with Bing Crosby, whom I like very much even although I only have a short chat with him. His manner is so pleasant, and he seems so quiet and non-aggressive. As our host must leave to meet his better half we leave too. Under no circumstance would he allow us to pay our own cover-charge — $3.50 per head!!

A man comes to me and asks me whether I have ever seen a broadcast. On answering to the negative he hands me two tickets for the NBC Broadcast at 11.15 pm. We have about 8 minutes to get there! I thank him very much find Wal in the crowd and go like hell for Radio City. Here I see the whole little game of putting on a radio show advertising Palmolive soap. It is very interesting and they certainly turn it on. Duke Ellington, whom we had seen a few minutes before, tears in, plays a number, and is off again — they never stop tearing about in New York day or night. At a quarter to twelve we are out. We drop into the Defence Services Club. Dance for an hour and are made very much at home. I like the place and want to stay but there is plenty of New York to see yet and it is only 1 am! (New York wakes up about this time.)

Sunday 20 June: Up at 9 am and have breakfast. New York is very busy, and it is very hot and humid. At the USO we get free tickets to a show on Broadway for the evening. Wal and I set off together again for the Empire State — the tallest building in the world 1250 feet high (102 stories). The lift ascends at 1800 ft per minute and half way we change lifts. As might be expected the view from the top is magnificent, unless you are above the clouds. It is clear today and I can see a hill far away, — all Manhattan is visible. It is almost lunch time when we have finished here — I am sure I could put a whole day in though! We dine with a couple of WAACs at the Automat Restaurant (help yourself).

We pick up Stan and George at Radio City in the Music Hall, a world famous building. We see a little of the stage show, which is extremely good, before Stan and I, sitting together, leave to see the interior of the Hall itself. Everything is black or mirror surfaces and diamond or right angle shaped — thus at once when you enter you are quiet and talk in soft tones or even a whisper, it seems so strange and extensive! This is just the effect they require and it is very effective. Soon we have Bettie and Margarette to contend with, and swap knowledge of our own countries. They come from White Plains, a little way out of New York, and seem decent, quite pleasant and reasonably intelligent. We find each other very interesting, and I learn a lot. I am amused at their expression 'solid' for anything that is extra good, and 'bloody sausage inbetweens' for Pork German sandwiches. We take them to the Waldorf Astoria for tea (or 'sawpper') and then to the show on Broadway, for we have 5 tickets between us, (the 5th I give to a Yank Marine). The show is 'As Time Goes By', and we all enjoy it very much. We take them by subway a hair-raising experience, to Grand Central and put them on their train — Goodnitch.

At something like 4.30 am we toddle into yet another night club where I get into conversation with a chap, just an ordinary type I think, but who turns out to be Mario Montealegre, Secretary of the Legation of Costa Rica, Wash. D.C. He takes us eventually to his apartment at Essex House, where we talk etc. until dawn — a most interesting and amusing bloke. Actually, before we met this Mario bloke who insisted on us calling him 'Monte', we dropped into the Astor Bar, in the Hotel Astor on Broadway. Here we get talking with some Yank Thunderbolt pilots, — first Yanks for whom I have had any time, and I find them most interesting. They expect to leave the States soon for service abroad. One of them, a young Lieutenant from a farm in Texas wangles us into the Astor Roof Garden where Harry James and his band are flat out. Here I meet his wife Betty Grable who is with Joan Bennett and others. This is the most wonderful dance floor I have ever seen (but I don't let on!). I wish I could have stayed longer here, but there is plenty of New York unseen yet.

At the Stage Door Canteen on 44th Street sometime later, we see Joan Bennett again with a relation of Gracie Fields — cousin I think. She gets amongst us and soon we are in her own private club, in 42nd Street. Here I meet the designer of the P-39 Airacobra. We go back to the Hotel Wentworth, 59 West 46th Street where we pick up Joan Bennett again, with her titanic Dalmatian on a red leash, and go for a short walk and odd sip here and there — 'So long boys, and good luck', are the words she leaves us with.

We go to sleep after leaving Monte at 9.30 am in Central Park!

Monday 21 June: New York to me has been a wonderful experience, but I should not like to live in the City. They say a New Yorker, once out of his own little neighbourhood is completely lost. I can well understand it. His knowledge of affairs in general is very limited — one of our chaps was even asked if he had come from Australia by car! Of course there are 9 million people in the city, all are not like this for there are bound to be some millions of good amongst the bad.

I have seen New York, I never want really to return, BY MYSELF. It is an island — a land indeed, of ultra modern folk living an ultra modern life of reckless fun, noise, speed and constant bustle, having everything they want right outside the front door. This is their life, and for this they will fight and indeed die. No doubt if I had been born and brought up here I would too, but I was not.

Sunday 27 June: The past few nights I have spent in Taunton and the other towns close by such as Providence, (where I saw the Andrew Sisters), Fall River, Brockton, Attleboro and even Boston which is quite some distance. I begin to stock up with things that I fear will be scarce in England. I have some 1400 razor blades, 2400 cigarettes, umpteen cakes of soap, tooth paste and brushes, chewing gum (2000 bits!!), and all sorts of muck. The 'Taunton Inn' I find very nice and spend some time there usually during an evening. Every night we have leave until 1 am, but sometimes the boys arrive home just in time for the 9 am parade! Last night I stayed in Camp and saw a stage show put on by the 'Camel Caravan' which tours the camps for Camel cigarettes. At the door they dish out 10 weeds apiece — the show was very good. I have taken numerous photos since arrival, and hope for good results.

Am very happy here, and very well — but Australia is still the best place on earth!

Tuesday 29 June: We are to leave in the morning. There is general panic. I have sent most of the stuff that I have bought home to Aussie, but still have Pat's watch and a couple of other things. America to me has been a grand adventure and a wonderful experience. I love the land but not the people. It is just their way I know, but still I cannot ever say, 'I like Americans'. If we Australians in Australia had what these Americans have, plus our own little lot, then surely Aussie would be paradise on earth.

Wednesday 30 June: We put on a show for the Yanks in the form of the march past. They are amazed, and so am I, for I have never been in a march before when the boys are turning it on like this. The Yank band play Waltzing Matilda which, by the way, I am weary of singing, for the American people really do love it. I think of home as they play it, and I realize now more than ever how far away I am.

Our train for New York leaves the siding at about 5 pm and most of the trip is in darkness. We have a slap up tea on the train. About midnight we get off the train and are ferried around to RMS 'Queen Elizabeth', on which I had a fair idea we would sail, for I had seen her in dock with 'Queen Mary', 'Aquatania' and others, whilst in New York. I can see the 'Normandie' lying on her side just like a huge toy boat. It must have been a terrific blaze of fire. There are houses built along her side — sleep on the job! Preparation for refloatation is almost complete. Just before we board 'Elizabeth', American Red Cross women come amongst us with doughnuts, lemon drink and chocolates. They are greatly appreciated — I shall never forget them, smiling, cheery and greyclad laughing and talking — it is about 2.15 am.

Once aboard and settled in, I go to bed and die!

PART 2

ENGLAND AND FAMILIARISATION

Thursday July 1 1943: We have left New York Harbour some time in the early hours of the morning and are out at sea. Blimps and Mitchells escort us. There are over 2,000 troops on board, most of them Americans, who get on our goat immediately. I have heard one say, 'this is our biggest boat!' — <u>our</u> boat mind you. She is an immense ship and goes like hell at some 36 knots (will do 42 flat out). I am sure that I shall lose myself before long — the most beautiful ship I've ever seen. Before lunch the gun crews let go for some practice and put on a fair show shooting clouds. The Yank niggers are scared to death.

While strolling down Port A deck I bang smack into my Thunderbolt pilot friend whom I met in the Astor Bar, New York. We are very surprised to see each other and have a long talk and arrange to meet again same place and time tomorrow. He is a regular guy and I like him. He is a bit upset because he has just missed seeing his first heir whom he expected any time — decidedly a poor show, because he will have to wait until he is in England, before he knows whether it is 'boy or girl' — Bill Nash is his name. He wants very much to see and fly a Spitfire.

Feel fine, there is hardly a move out of Lizzie and the Atlantic is very calm although the weather is crook. We steer a zig-zag course.

Sunday 4 July: Just found out that beer is available on board, but I cannot for the life of me navigate myself to where it is, no matter how good the instructions may be.

Monday 5 July: Met at sea by two long range Spitfires (from a carrier no doubt), a Liberator and a Sunderland. Some time during the night it is known we successfully avoided several U boats. Some of the chaps who were awake felt the acute turns and course alterations, also the increased speed, and 'action station' alert. The anti-sub apparatus they have, I am told, is amazing. They can pick up even a wooden box floating on the surface at unbelievable range.

We are each given 6 tins of American rations — evidently we're going somewhere where we'll be a little peckish when we land — reputed to be tomorrow evening or the next day.

Tuesday 6 July: We sight the northern coast of Ireland and I believe parts of Scotland. There is great excitement. All day aircraft, mostly Spitfires (together with Hurricanes, Scuas, Beaufighters and Sunderlands) are above us. We cause a great deal of panic to the Yanks now, slinging off at P-40s, 38s, 39s, 47s etc. and they are a little hostile. In the Firth of Clyde I see the aircraft carrier 'Illustrious' which has seen so much action in the Mediterranean theatre. I find it hard to believe that this little green land I can see is Scotland. I keep watching it glide by. There are some really pretty little places even here. At length we drop anchor some hundred yards from shore off Grenock. We are told where each of us is going, during the course of a lecture by some RAF type. I am Brighton bound, on the south east coast somewhere. There is plenty of panic tonight.

Wednesday 7 July: All morning and indeed all afternoon Yanks are unloaded and at 8 pm in bright daylight still, we finally get aboard a ferry and push off from Lizzy, which now towers above us in her dirty grey war paint. I write my name and home address on her side in pencil, plus 'You big beaut!'

And so I set foot on Scotland, a little bewildered at its strangeness, and I suppose, by the fact that this is really it. Soon, however we are on the move again in a funny little train. We are given bread and tea (Hm! this is where our tinned food comes in and, we fall back on a little of our chocolate reserves). I look out the window trying to take it all in. I see tiny cottages and little fields, hedges and rock-fences, long rows of brick homes, men and women, children too, poorly clad wave to us with the Victory and Thumbs Up signs. Everything seems so small, dingy and pokey — and damp. I suppose we shall get used to it. Dusk falls and I am still quite silent and still a little puzzled. How strange it all is. We have to put the black-outs down in the train. This is getting too fair-dinkum. I go into a little passageway in the dark and look out there. I see two beautiful streams at quite close intervals and in each a couple of rings where a trout has risen, and decide to get amongst these some day soon, if possible.

Although we have not done much in the past 24 hours, what we have done has tired us out and at about 11 pm I decide to go to sleep, but it is not until shortly after 1 am, just after passing through Carlisle, that I get to sleep.

Thursday 8 July: I have slept well and awake just in time to see a little of the outskirts of London. At once I notice the shabbiness of it all. Everything needs a coat of paint. Here and there I see evidence of bombing. There are barrage balloons above. Still I see these long lines of little brick homes, in which I feel sure just by looking at them live hard-working people, men, women, and children who in a time of awful tragedy can fall back, not on tears — but on laughter. What a tremendous fund of public spirit there must be. 'So this is England', I keep saying to myself. On the face of it I do not like it already, but I am proud of it.

Past London we get into a little country which I like the look of. It is very like Tasmania here really. I have seen numerous aerodromes and numerous aircraft types which I have not seen before. Down into Sussex which I like the look of, because I suppose, this is countryside I am looking at. It is all green — a wandering greenness, here and there I see a little hamlet in amongst the trees, and always there is a church spire. And so at length we detrain at Brighton on the coast at about 1.15 pm. For a short time, until we are all sorted out, we are billeted in the biggest hotels in the town. I am on the third floor of the Metropole Hotel, right on the sea front, facing France!

Out I go to give Brighton the once over. First thing of importance I find out is that there are almost 500 pubs in the town — that's a good show, almost one each! Second I find that Jerry frequently comes over here during daylight as well as night on nuisance raids. Secretly I wish he'd come right now as I am dying to see a crate with black crosses on it! I am most annoyed inwardly when late in the evening we have an alert, but no pips (these being somewhat like a radio time signal and denoting aircraft overhead).

Brighton is a town of some considerable size and I believe during peacetime is a popular seaside holiday resort. Now it is rather shabby as might be expected. The beach is littered with wreckage of both aircraft and vessels and old buoys, exploded mines — all manner of junk. There are huge barb wire structures and anti tank and landing barge traps along its entire length preventing anyone going near the beach, (in any case it is heavily mined).

Friday 9 July: Jerry is over today and wallops a cinema at East Grenstead where five WAAFs are killed. Two DO217E2s are shot down. I exchange what American money I have left for English — $4 to the pound.

Here I am gaining my first impression of the English people and England herself. It is not too good. Admittedly they have had several years of war. I admire them for the way they have stuck that. I find Tamplin's Brown Ale about the best or India Pale Ale (8p a glass).

Saturday 17 July: For the past week I have been more or less constantly on the go with a surprising amount of red tape and messing about. At last it seems that we have finished with it. I know Brighton well now and am quite satisfied with the place. The weather has been quite nice with sunshine and it is very pleasant out. When there is time a few of us climb aboard a bus and go for short trips around Brighton, to Patcham, Rottingdean, Shoreham, Old Steyning and many little places close by, for this is the only England I like — the outdoor England. We have been having lectures lately regarding flying in this country as compared with in Australia, what we shall find strange and so on. We have numerous alerts, often between 12.30 am and 1 pm. He seems to come in low at Beachy Head turn left inland a little way and sweep down over and behind Brighton letting his bombs go at a very low level anywhere. There is very little notice taken of him except for a few words. Of course some damage is always done and there are always lives lost.

The war is here alright. And yet the people I see around me go about their work with very little ado, the dances seem just as peace-time-like and the cinemas no different. In the pubs there is an odd word of war, but not much. They seem to have outwardly forgotten the war but they have not in their hearts. They are aiming to finish it once and for all this time. I seem always to be in need of money! We are on English Currency now and our money does not go as far. However I am learning to spend the English way.

Actually I had expected to find a badly wounded England — the place bombed almost flat, but here in Brighton for instance there is not that much damage. In any case half the places could do with a stick of heavies across them! I do not like the English custom of adding little pieces to a building every so often. In some cases one part may be almost at the crumbling stage, while another is newly-built and modern! I find the amount of food and clothing to be had a great surprise also. Of course the rationing system is strict, but they do alright. Such commodities as eggs, butter, jam, sugar, tea, canned fruit and fresh fruit and meat seem the most heavily rationed and also the most scarce. Everyone has enough to live, that it the main thing.

The blackout is very strict quite naturally. We cannot smoke near the waterfront after dark and must return to the hotel by a special route. This is a little difficult for the boys if they have had a heavy night! As many people have 'gone bush' from here, flats and apartments are most numerous. Some of the boys have their own flat — good idea! (I share one with two others at 19/6 a week! Here we sometimes knock up a feed of fried bread, tomatoes and margarine — also bacon if possible, at unearthly hours in the morning.)

Friday 23 July: I have been before a Selection Board for the purpose of deciding what aircraft I am to fly and after pleading for half an hour for Mustangs in Tactical Air Force and being given daylight Spits in Fighter Command, I am not very displeased because a lot of chaps who trained on singles, have been put on multies. The demand for bomber pilots is acute and if they can see any way out, then you're a gonner and a bomber pilot! I am told it may be three months before I get onto fighters, but I should wait three years. However I shall be posted from here, before AFU, to various airfields to learn a little of the difficulties in flying in this country and also for experience.

I have been given leave from 26th to 31st of this month, and having seen Lady Francis Ryder, who does a wonderful job for the Air Force getting people who are willing to take a couple of chaps in, where they will be most suited and happy, I am to go with another pilot Harry Jenson from Sydney, whom I have become good friends with, to Oxford where we will stay with a Dr & Mrs Gurney.

We have had numerous raids and alerts, but no bombs have fallen close enough to me yet to scare the daylights out of me. I enjoy these raids very much! especially when they begin pumping the flak up. There is no better way of describing the noise it makes, than the word 'crump'! I have taken several more bus rides, a little further afield than before, and visit Alfriston a beautiful little place with a tumbled down church and a handful of people, Lewes, Berwick, Pyecombe, Worthing, Peacehaven and others all of which I find very interesting and beautiful in their own little way. I take numerous photographs, but can see that soon I shall be up the spout for film.

Out towards Berwick, Stan Silver and I find ourselves near a little church one sunny afternoon. Inside we find the vicar and have a long talk with him. It is not bomb-blast that has shaken the building, but about six months ago the field artillery had been practicing in the neighbouring fields and the shock from the guns had caused some damage. The church had been first built in about 1400, but in true English fashion additions here and there had taken place including the spire some 800 years ago! This is old — I have seen many churches and all of them are very old.

At times I have been a little browned off with things in general. I am sure a bit of mail would help matters. I frequent the Regent Dance Hall and the various cinemas to pass time.

One afternoon I met a girl named Helen and we talked on a wooden seat before having fish 'n chips in the park. Towards evening she showed me an air raid shelter. After a while I go to check on some kids outside and on return find her lying on the low flat table naked from the waist down.

This is my first encounter with a prostitute and having just been lectured a couple of days ago about the risk of catching a dose, I tell her I have to get back to camp where I get pretty mad on finding my wallet stolen from my tunic top pocket while I was checking outside.

Monday 26 July: Set off on leave to Oxford. All I see of London is the view from the window of one of the funny little, rattling, ancient London taxi-cabs with an old hand-horn, — horrible looking things. However I go from Victoria Station to Paddington Station and during the ride I see London in its very dirty war-paint. Everything is shabby and needs paint. Here and there I see evidence of bombs and fire, there are great holes and blast pittings in the walls. At very frequent intervals there are huge water tanks built of steel on the roadside for use in case of fire (these are in Brighton also). I am entirely lost, as in New York. There are many civilians about, but I suppose they all have war work of some kind. There are countless double-decker buses, red and white or green in colour mostly. The entire city is covered by an immense balloon barrage, usually being moored in some open land — the results of direct hits I take it.

From Paddington I catch my train, and after changing at Reading, quite a town, I arrive at Oxford late in the afternoon. The trip had been most interesting for I had covered a considerable amount of country and there was lots to see.

I find that I shall not spend my leave in Oxford but a little way out, some 6 miles at a district named Boar's Hill. Harry, who had left the day before meets me at the station and we taxi out. The home, named 'Bayworth Corner', is a lovely old English place covered almost entirely with ivy and after meeting Dr & Mrs Gurney I am sure that I am to enjoy myself. The doctor is very interested in Botany and his wife in foreign languages. They have a son in Tunisia.

It is tea time when I have unpacked and changed, and what a tea! The large bottle of Woodpecker Cider improves things too. After tea Harry and I take a little toddle down the road to The Fox and Hounds, stay a while before returning, and stroll back across the fields.

Thursday 29 July: The last couple of days I have spent mostly in Oxford. Here again I am struck by the shabbiness and dustiness of the places. I find the colleges, and there are many, of great historic interest. Inside Oxford cathedral I touch stone which was laid about 780 AD and here also I see famous tombs mutilated and defaced, I am told by Cromwell and his followers. Dr Gurney certainly knows his stuff in this direction too, and gives us all the gen imaginable.

It is very hot in the sun about midday. Once we took a boat and went down the Thames a short way. Here under the willows we found it quiet and cool. I have met Prof Murray, the celebrated Egyptologist — an amazing person! He, Dr Gurney, a Prof in Forestry and I go walking in a wood one afternoon. Here I am further amazed by the amount of knowledge these two have. I am sure either one of them could talk for days on a single leaf!

I am having a whale of a time. At 8.30 am the maid (one of them that is) wakes me and at 9.15 <u>sharp</u>, the breakfast gong goes and wow! — nobody is more that 20 seconds late. I have a huge double bed to myself and I make the most of it.

Saturday 31 July: We go into town in the late evening and get all mixed up with a Scotch family who eventually, after taking us to their home for tea, take us across the fields to Trout Inn, Godstow. This is a famous little place, many noted personages having been here at different times. The interior is decorated with knives, mugs, cups, swords, guns and pistols indeed every flaming thing possible — even butterflies and stuffed birds, fish and animals. I decided then and there that I would return there today to get a couple of photographs, (which I did on the doc's bike!) We have a couple of pints here at Trout Inn and walk through the little garden of roses beside the stream. There are several peacocks in the garden.

At length we return to their home for supper, and talk about trout, for they are a great trouting family. I learn a few good haunts, one especially recommended is Lake Vyrnivy in Wales, via Oswespry. Here I am told, good sport with the dry (Beetles and Midges I expect) is to be had. There are plenty fish although they do not run to any size.

I have spent a very pleasant leave here and like Dr & Mrs Gurney very much. Nothing is a bother to them, they are kind and generous (they have two little boys who have lost their all in London during the Blitz — Peter and John. Mrs Gurney is a real mother to them. I don't think they really know what happened to their real mother). There is never any trouble in the running of the house. Always there are happy faces, always there are kind words. This is a different England to me again. We have had an alert at exactly 1.05 am for the last two mornings, but no bombs have fallen near us. It is the Thames Estuary and parts of the home counties that get it.

I am distinctly a little sad when I say goodbye to these two dear people. I promise to write to them and tell them all that befalls me. I shall never forget the old Doctor and his old Englishman manner, his 'bother the jolly thing', his 'wretched ado' and so on. They really have a lovely home and it suits them both. And so I leave them standing waving at the gate as I move off on the bus which will take me to Oxford Carfax. It is mid afternoon, the sun is out and England now looks lovely in its greenery of oaks, birches, plane trees, chestnut trees and the little green fields with hedges around the edges. Oats is growing in some fields. It seems almost ready for harvest. Can there really be a war on?

The trip back to London is uneventful. At Paddington a little poorly-clad man, full of energy, runs up to me 'Taxi Aussie?' I give him half a crown for his trouble and soon I am well on the way to Victoria Station. I arrive back in Brighton, after another uneventful journey of some hour and a half, — quite interesting though, just in time for an alert, but still no bombs land near me!

Saturday 7 August: We have begun a series of lectures which will last three weeks all to do with flying naturally. The most interesting lecturer I find is a F/Lt Payne, a fighter pilot back from Middle East who has six confirmed victories.

I have contacted Arthur Plant my old Eildon Weir trout fisher friend who is over here with the AIF Forestry Unit now stationed near Horsham in Sussex. It appears he is soon to return to Australia. I wish I had kept Pat's watch now, for here is the perfect chance. However I suppose it will be alright with F/Lt Cook. I must arrange to meet him soon.

By now I have become quite used to the countless aircraft overhead and only look up sometimes at dusk when hundreds of bombers set off across the channel for the targets. Sometimes they will take an hour or more to pass over. I always wish them luck. Secretly I admire these blokes.

I realize now more fully that although my life is but young yet, that I have had a wonderful home, and I appreciate how much those at home have done for me to make this young life that I have led so wonderful. Where would I be only for them? Every single thing good that I have experienced I can trace back to this. They have given and shown me a great life, if anything should happen to me while I am away, all that they have done will not have been in vain. If we should fail to win this struggle, then lives like mine might not be possible. To me this means a great deal.

We all still find England and English ways a little strange and even a little objectionable — perhaps a little more than before. There is too much class distinction. The people themselves admit this. I realize they have been at war for a long time and that their way of life is somewhat warped, but it is the very things they fight for that are strange to us — their freedom, their fun, their free speech for all, and the rest of it. These are all different ideas in the two opinions — ours and theirs. And again, we are just colonials, just the dirt about the place and we must do what the people of England do, if we want to be truly a free people! How many times have I had staggering looks when I say, 'Listen mate', to some dear, dear Limey, 'I, and these other blokes, don't give so much as a damm what the English people say, do or think. We are Australians, — and that alone makes us the luckiest people on earth'.

One afternoon I go by bus to Eastbourne (East along the coast from Brighton). Here I find that Jerry has landed a few bombs, both recently and in the early days. Recently Woolworth's has had it, also Barclay's Bank, the fire station, the Art School, several churches, numerous homes, the station and numerous other places. There are vacant blocks here and there where bombs have fallen in the Blitz days. I am told that a FW190 machine gunned the streets from a low level a few days ago, killing and wounding a number of people. He was brought down in a field by light ack-ack.

Another afternoon I bus my way to Hastings, about the size of Eastbourne. (5/8/43.) Here they have had one or two sticks too. I am just leaving Lyons Cafe, when I hear an aircraft pass at terrific speed overhead. It brushes over the chimneys with a terrific roar and vanishes, heading towards the sea. Almost immediately a Spit 5 B followed later by another, disappear in the same direction. The first A/C was an ME109 quite out of control, which the Spits had shot down. It hit the water and blew up some five miles out to sea yet it passed overhead at no more than 150 feet! A little bit lower, and I would certainly have had my finger out.

I find the houses out towards Patcham very beautiful and twice now I have gone out after tea in the long cool evening and sketched a few of them. I plan to send these home. A pound of grapes is worth usually between 17/- and 19/- sometimes more, and a single peach up to 7/- or 8/-. We find it almost unbelievable! Fresh fruit of any kind is very scarce. I have many late nights and getting up in the mornings I find a bit of a bind. We have been in this country just a month now. It is about two and a half months since I left home. It seems like years.

Thursday 12 August: Things are about the same. No mail yet which is my biggest moan.

We have had several raids at night of late, and I find these great sport. Some of the chaps treat the alerts with respect and lose no time getting under cover. Just the same if you're going to go for a row, you'll go, shelter or no shelter, so I take these opportunities of seeing the works as it happens. If it's cold we don't even get out of bed to have a look — a standard joke is going around, I'm not getting out of bed for any Jerry!

It seems to me that the invasion of the continent will not be long now. Army, Navy and Air Force are constantly doing manoeuvres. Nobody talks much, but it looks a bit this way to me. The countless Canadians who have been stationed round about are beginning to move away — where I have no idea. I can pass hours away very happily simply wandering around the quaint old shops. True I spend this way, but I have not bought anything valueless, or without some particular interest. No doubt I shall have a suit-case full of junk when the time comes to go home. I never get up for breakfast now and to make up for it I enlarge the morning tea at the 'Black Cat' in Ship Street.

Tuesday 17 August: (2 raiders brought down last night, 6 night before.) I set off again soon after breakfast for Friston where I learn the cockpit drill on the Spit 5 B and II. I go for a short flip in a Tiger with a Polish chap named Orbech. Although these chaps are noted for rough and disorderly behaviour, they are also noted for having done some very fine flying. I admire each and every one of them, not so much for what he is, but for what he has gone through. For example this chap with whom I fly, knows that his father was beheaded, has no idea where has mother is, and that his only sister has been taken by officers as a comfort. His home is burnt to the ground — a typical example. After having spoken to quite some number of Poles I find that they fear the Russians a great deal and will not trust them. They seem sure that before Spring the Russians will have pushed back past Poland into Germany and that Poland will remain under Russian domination — makes you think!

Saturday 21 August: Soon after 10 am I go to Gatwick. Here I fly in a Master III and a Halifax II. The Master is a nice A/C with a roomy and well set-out cockpit. I find it much the same as a Wirra and am eager to get to an AFU on them. The Halifax is a truly wonderful A/C, more like a flying hotel but I should not like to fly one, because I have no interest in these big A/C — besides you can't fly it upside-down! Here I have the first opportunity of looking the Mustang, Typhoon and Tomahawk over and spend some time playing around in all of them. On the station there are also Wellingtons and Whitleys.

The past few days have been cold, wet and miserable, so most of my time has been spent indoors writing and drawing. We have had a couple of raids by small numbers of DO217E2 dive bombers. Some damage is done and a number of people killed and injured. Eastbourne and Caterham get a walloping.

There is almost a shuttle service of our aircraft across the channel all day and night. Huge formations of Forts, sometimes escorted by Spits and 47s, go over in the mornings. Bostons, Mitchells and Marauders attack their targets in the afternoon and at night the heavies Lancs, Halys, Stirlings etc. give him hell. Fighter Command have lately staged some of the biggest sweeps for the year — indeed the War. I counted 290 Spits one day last week.

Back in July (Sunday 25th) Bomber Command began a terrific bombardment of Europe. Essen Cologne, Le Harve, Remsheid, Nuremburg, Duisberg and Hamburg get a hell of a plastering. On 27th July Hamburg was almost wiped clean out. These raids usually only cost between about eighteen and thirty five A/C which is very small considering the number over the target. In daylight the Forts concentrate on airfields and aircraft plants etc. They often visit Abbeville Poix, Merville, Tricquelle, Kassel, Kiel, Oschersleben, Wessermunde, Wilhemshaven, Courtrai, Rostock, Hamburg, St Omer, Bordeaux, Martin, Schweinfurt, Amiens, Vitry en Artois, Amiens-Glisy, Flushing and countless other targets.

This bomber offensive is increasing daily. Comparing this with the hammering Britain got in 1940 — England has not been scratched yet!

An alert is sounded soon after I leave the Agg's place at about 2350 hours. I can hear him coming soon — there doesn't seem many of them. They are not high, about 6 thou'; and it is a clear bright moonlight night. Up goes the flak. They avoid it, and pass on to bomb the outskirts of London. There is damage, and casualties are quite heavy. Two of them are shot down by Beaufighters. I hear them go out across the coast later on. They dive down to sea level. One drops a flare as he passes the coast. No doubt Mossies will follow them home.

Monday 23 August: At 1125 hours I get my first letter from home. It is written just before I left 2ED. This is a real surprise and I decide to celebrate for I am happy. Surely there must be more where this comes from so there is bound to be one from Pat. I shall die if there isn't. Soon after tea I bus out to Rottingdean, right on the coast. Here I stand at the edge of the cliff — white chalk cliffs, and look out to sea. It is only about 8 minutes by crate to France across there! I can hear the heavy guns at Dover (and nearer) sending a few shells across.

In Brighton the alert goes and immediately they are here. Searchlights are on the job and I see a couple of planes — DO217s I think, weaving to get out of the beams. Flak goes up like hell. There are flashes from bombs both East and West but none here yet. Worthing and Peacehaven — invasion ports? are getting it. Next minute a crate comes across overhead. I can tell it to be Jerry by the motors. A Mossie is after him and lets go with cannon — misses. Jerry turns right, dives and, bingo, I'm up in the air and down again in a heap in a park! The explosion was terrific. I cannot hear. (I saw green, blue, red and orange flame — I think). I get up. The Mossie is at it again with cannon and m/g now. There is a spurt of flame from Jerry, and down he goes into the sea not far from the shore to explode like a huge cracker. I can see another going down towards Worthing. They are getting it badly down there, about 20 bombs have fallen. There is a huge pall of dust and smoke around where I am. I look up the street. Already firemen, wardens etc. are on the job and have a rope across the road. I am not wanted so set off to see what's left of the hotel! In about 20 mins the all clear goes, only to be followed by another alert. This is wonderful fun. I still can't hear! I have a tear in my pants and a cut hand.

I see a FW190 quite plainly against the moon flying at some 150 ft along the waterfront. A Mossie follows soon in the same direction, nav. lights on and flashing the colours of the period to the gunners. (A Mossie was shot down not long ago here in broad daylight!) Back at the billet the boys tell me more than two are down. I have a beer, a smoke, write a letter, and go to bed.

Sunday 29 August: After lunch I go by train to Ford, a Beaufighter, Mosquito and FAA station. I am amazed at the damage which a Stirling and Halifax have sustained during the raid on Nuremburg last night, and still returned to England — although they only just made it. The Stirling has 209 bullet holes in it, the outboard port motor U/S, a 3-4 ft hole in the port wing and another in the rudder, the port flap gone, the nose shattered and generally bent. The Halifax has no port outboard and only about 3 ft of the blades left on the port inner airscrew, a huge hole in the port elevator and the rear turret smashed, about a 4 ft hole on the starboard side of the fuselage a flat starb'd tyre, and no hydraulic power!

I fly in a Mosquito II with an Australian P/O Jackson. (Cruise at 300 on port motor, 485-490 in shallow dive, approach at 180 stall at 100-105, enter circuit at 190 with flap to reduce speed). We go far out to sea and back inland around Arundel. We shoot up a golf course at 480 mph. I am absolutely amazed. It is a truly beautiful A/C. He has been over Germany only 7 times. He is going again tonight. The apparatus IFF, 'G', 'D', AIU etc. I find astounding. I cannot write what little I know of it here even. This is real gen. His experiences are most interesting. I do a circuit in a Lancaster, together with its full crew. They only just made it back here from Nuremburg about a week ago. The pilot is a F/S — GT of RNZAF They are a wonderful job. I return to Brighton have a snack and go to a show at the Princess, 'Elizabeth and Essex.'

Monday 30 August: There was a short alert early this morning (about 3.20 am but no aircraft came here, London has a couple of eggs. 11 dead.) I get the first news from Pat in a telegram. This is a happy day and calls for celebration. I wire back immediately, also home. After lunch I go to Shoreham where I fly in a Lysander and a Walrus. In the Duck we go a long way out across the Channel. France any minute now I think! We land and take off from the water, fly back a good way inland and return. After tea I <u>certainly do celebrate</u>.

Total losses in the air war to dawn 29th August:

	Axis:	Allies:
A/C destroyed in air or ack ack:	16,437	11,104
Personnel:	37,278	42,531

Excluding Russia and Far East.

Saturday 4 September: I note that the Spit 5Cs now in Australia are quoted by AM to have a top speed of 369 at 19,500 and reaches 30,000 ft in 13 minutes — not good enough.

I get a letter from Arthur Plant, who has been on leave. I hope to see him next weekend. He has got me an invitation to do some fishing and shooting in Scotland on some huge Estate — good show! After dinner I go out to Haywards Heath with Wal Summerton and Dave Ryan. At a cricket match we meet an AIF chum. (He knows Arthur Plant.) I take some photos.

While walking down the road we are picked up in a car by a Major Desmond Patrick Flynn and one of his adopted sons (Navy). He takes us to his lovely home in Balcombe. He is a most interesting man and most amusing — although Irish, very English. The house is full of historic interest, the dining room table for instance is hundreds of years old and must be 30 ft long and 4 ft wide! The walls are armed with shields, arrows, bows, swords, guns etc. We have tea, eat tomatoes, smoke and learn archery. I am in a talking mood and we two get along fine when I begin telling him what's wrong with England! He drives me to Lady & Sir Reginald Blaker's place we collect his nephews and return for tea, after which we go into long interesting talk about England. I learn a lot. (He went to Dunkirk in a 16 ft launch!) We take the nephews back about 10 pm. He has another drink or two and finds driving a little awkward for his first start is in reverse, his second with the brakes on. I have a go and finish up in a holly hedge. We get back whole, and talk more. Eventually we catch the last train to Brighton

11.58 pm. I shall never forget this night. Actually incidents like this have been quite numerous since arrival in this country, but after America I am quite used to it and take it all as a matter of course. I have had a lot of amusing times. Tonight I have enjoyed a great deal. He used to have two Aussies staying at his place every leave. They both have gone for a burton now. He insists that I visit him again some time, I only hope I can. I promise to anyway!

Sunday 5 September: I think I have visited about a third of the 500 pubs in Brighton. I have been in all the cinemas, theatres and dance halls. I know my way about pretty well. I have never been in an air raid shelter yet! Our chocolate ration is 1–3 bar per week, but we can get a little ration free stuff at a little Canadian Legion place. Not all the blokes know of it, which is fortunate. After lunch I go by train to Arundel where there is a huge castle perched on the summit of a hill surrounded on all sides by tall green trees. On the east side is a lake, with green lawns around the edges. Here I take some good photos which I shall send home. I find it very interesting. Instead of returning by train I throw away the return ticket and catch a bus which takes a roundabout route (taking some 2 hours) giving me a good opportunity of seeing a bit more of Sussex.

Sunday 12 September: This is the last straw. My browning off process has come to a climax. I'm charcoal black — we're all, the whole lot of us except one who have been posted, without warning, to an Oxford AFU! Hell!! For a moment I couldn't believe it when the names appeared. Slowly it sunk in and I think now I fully realize what this means — simply that I am one of many mugs. I am too disappointed and dejected to do more than laugh and joke about it.

After lunch I go to Horsham in search of Arthur Plant. Finally, after some hours messing about, we discover each other and have a long talk and a couple, at the Railway Inn at Horsham. He will take a parcel back for Pat, and some letters (one home and one to Pat). He expects to leave in a few days time and is very excited to be going home — who wouldn't? We are very pleased to meet each other after so long. We have so much to say and no time to say it. At 2017 hours he catches his train and at 2019 I catch mine. I am so glad that I have seen him. I only wish that I had kept Pat's watch and given it to him — I could kick myself, but how did I know?

Back in Brighton I have a little strife getting through the barrier — (they have placed a ban here and at other 'invasion points'? prohibiting entry to any who do not live here. A great many have been sent away also, all along the coast — any time now is the general opinion. There is constant landing barge activity in the channel.)

At one of our haunts I find a great many of the singles chaps drowning their sorrows, and so I join them. We leave in various shapes and forms and once back at the Met we set about wrecking the place, and it's no half job. The boys don't at all like the idea of multies! There is hardly a bucket of sand upright, a fire extinguisher serviceable. The dust bins and waste paper salvage receptacles have all gone out the windows, also the notice boards, in the first five minutes. It is a real good show after a while.

PART 3

CONVERSION TO BOMBERS

Tuesday 14 September: We catch our train, and have about an hour in London before getting the Rugby train. The trip is quite interesting and takes 2½ hours. At length we arrive at Church Lawford having been driven from Rugby some five miles to the drome. On seeing the Oxfords I am wilder than ever, and am considering refusing straight out to fly 'em. We settle in okay I suppose. This would be a super station if it had Masters on it! We are to camp in Nissen huts for a while. I have always wanted to sleep in one of these turnouts. They look so cosy to me. I find Sgt's Mess very nice — plenty tables, chairs etc. Two huge fire places are a good sign. There are also darts, billiards, wireless — and of course a good looking bar.

Friday 17 September: Our course is to consist of 2 weeks lectures, 2 weeks lectures and flying, 2 weeks flying, 1 week of Bat, 2 weeks night flying and another 2 weeks daylight flying. Then Reserve Flight flying. I find the station very good and am sure I'll be happy here.

Have met a pilot Ron Dent of RNZAF and we are already good friends. We have much the same interests, and both are all out for fighters. Already we have made our objections to multies known to all and sundry and there seems to be a spark of hope that we shall get what we want. It has been done before. I have taken up biting my finger nails again over this problem — I don't want to either sleep or eat. All we can do is talk of some way to get onto singles.

Monday 20 September: We have decided to go to London to RAAF HQ — Air Ministry if necessary to see about singles. We'll leave here on Friday afternoon.

It is a good Mess the food being good (and the beer!). Actually its a good camp — the only trouble is singles! We have taken a distinct dislike to a lot of 'Limies' about the place, and a distinct liking to some Canadian chaps.

Friday 24 September: Ron Dent, Tom Noon, Mac Kennedy and myself set off for London. The train trip is terrible and after two and three quarter hours we reach London (about 10.30 pm) very browned off. We ring numerous places for a bed, starting off posh with the Regent and Strand Palace etc., finally very humbly accepting a bed at the Church Army Hostel for 1/- a night! Accommodation in London we have now learnt, is 'ard to git. About midnight, after a toddle around Piccadilly and a couple of jugs, we arrive there and soon we are in bed — <u>very</u> comfortable beds at that.

Saturday 25 September: About 0930 we arise and without breakfast go straight to Kodak House, Kingsway where I interview a P/O Thomas, who hears me sympathetically, and suggests we see a F/Lt Long at FTHQ Reading! (RAAF Liaison Officer). We decide to go. At 1445 we catch a train from Paddington to Reading — some 1½ hours journey. We taxi out to FTHQ go through all the bullo and find our man not at home. This is almost the last straw! However we see the Adjutant, who suggests we write to him, and tells us that he will inform him of our visit on return. He thinks F/Lt Long may even fly up to Church Lawford to see us. We leave not in the best of humour — very fed up with England in any shape or form.

Sunday 26 September: Today throughout Britain there are countless services in memory of the Battle of Britain. Yesterday in London I saw preparations for the huge march past Buckingham Palace. (Here I saw Mr Churchill for the first time — just as I pictured he would be in reality, strong and resolute. Even at sight he is inspiring. Here is one Englishman I admire and praise.)

We put on a show in Rugby. The march is quite good and the service also. The Army, Navy, ATS, WRENS etc. are all represented. I am proud to be taking part in a service in commemoration of such fine deeds as those done by such fine chaps in those hard days. That I might have shared their task is one of my greatest disappointments. And now that there is doubt as to whether I can follow on in their footsteps with Fighter Command, today I feel very browned off. I have even said aloud such thoughtless things as I would like to see another large scale bombing of Britain so that fighter pilots would again be needed urgently! The whole trouble is that I am three years too late, or three years too young or somim! Today is a great day indeed for the people of England and Fighter Command.

Wednesday 29 September: I commence flying today — what a thrill! I make an awful song about how I hate multies.

Last night 2015 hrs a roar overhead and we thought our roof had gone. Next thing the motors went and bump. One of our boys missed out on a take-off, had engine failure or something and pranged in the valley about 100 yds from here. You've never seen such a mess. Bits of kite everywhere. The bloke was Allison from WA Don't know whether I knew him or not, I'm wondering what tonight will bring forth. We shall see.

Sunday 3 October: I have had a couple of hours in these flying matchboxes and today they let me breeze off solo — something I am not proud of. I am indeed sorry for the chaps I knew at the Junction who went to Oxboxes at Cook. These are not crates at all — just wallowing, slow, clumsy, toy-like, flimsy guts-breakers. I'll slow roll one of them yet.

Saturday 9 October: Two bombers were destroyed over East Anglia last night. Bombs dropped killed some 20 persons.

(Losses to dawn October 10th)

	Axis	Allies
A/C	17,693	11,945
Personnel	38,792	46,914

(Official A.M. Figures)
Excluding Russia and Far East
Makes you think doesn't it!

After tea Ron, Tom, Norm Hewitt (RNZAF) and I go to Bilton a little hamlet nearby where we have a merry time at the Black Horse Inn until closing time (10.30 pm). We find the place chokablock full of people, a seat is utterly out of the question. The beer and drinks are good. Just before closing we slip across the road to The Crown for another couple. This is not a young folk's 'ouse and all the old gentlemen of Bilton are here talking like fury. Dunchurch and Long Lawford are also little towns within close proximity of the camp and at Long Lawford the New Inn is quite popular because of the potato chips obtainable there. A little way along the Coventry road there is what I have learned to call Greasy Joe's, a minute shop where the boys sometimes go for hot snags, spuds and bacon for supper.

I find a great deal of pleasure and fun in these little nocturnal wanderings of ours. I have been poaching once also with some local village boys. I have also been in numerous apple orchards during the darker hours — one little party arrived home with a fine pair of chickens one night! I am all for a little fun like this — why not?

Wednesday 13 October: Last night during slight enemy air activity over South East England, one raider was brought down. It crashed in a street and blew up doing considerable damage.

We have experienced our first fogs in England. This morning it was particularly heavy and vision was almost nil. Flying, except Bat, was impracticable. I found the instructors very decent with one exception — this F/O Harpham I cannot quite make out. I have flown around the place a bit now and then and have been over Birmingham, Coventry, Wolverhampton, Leamington, Warwick, Kidlington, Northhampton and a few other large towns. The 'Day-night' flying I find most weird. (We fly with very dark glasses making things blacker than night. The 'flare Path' is illuminated by sodium flares. For a while I didn't know whether I was bald punched or Good Friday!)

Sunday 17 October: Today I go for a X-country flip which I find most pleasant and interesting. The track takes me from base to Stow-in-the-Wold, just north of Little Rissington. It is a peculiar little town made entirely of local creamish stone. There are six roads leading into it giving it the appearance of a huge spider. From here across to Olney where I get horribly tangled up amongst some 190 odd Forts returning from a raid. From here up to Oakham (I pass just east of Northampton). Oakham is west nor'west from Peterborough which I decide, from the huge columns of smoke and the dirty haze, is a large industrial town. The last leg home is into the sun and this makes everything a little difficult. Throughout the whole trip I constantly alter course to avoid other crates — Lancs, Halys, Stirlings, Spits, Forts, Mossies, Tiffs, Beauies, Wimps, Masters, Hurries — indeed almost every type in service! I have found this A/C avoiding business a nightmare. The sky is always full of kites all going in different directions at different heights and speeds. A constant watch must be kept. I am surprised that more do not collide.

Monday 18 October: Three enemy A/C destroyed last night. Some came as far in as Northampton causing our night flying to be called off for a while.

I am now firmly convinced that I cannot quite appreciate or understand England. There are fine things here, great and beautiful things and there are some lovely people here. But to me, indeed 'us' a great many things seem cockeyed. I doubt whether I shall ever understand England. I once went into a house in London where an old gentleman — only 86, and his wife lived. Bombs had fallen all about the place and there were no window panes and no ceilings with plaster on them. The old man took me upstairs finally, for he was conducting a tour of the little shattered home. 'An incendiary came through the roof here,' he would say, 'and the blast from an HE across the road blew this in' and so on. At length he showed me the bathroom and toilet and went to great lengths to explain how the cistern worked, when it did, and how after turning this, pushing that, waiting until so and so happened, pulling this out, twisting that — would I believe it in fifteen minutes there would be enough hot water in the bath for the purpose. 'No?' I said. 'Yes'! he replied, and a moment later, 'why, haven't you got things like this in Australia?' — Hell.

I find it an amazing thing that only about one in fifty toilets in England work, whether you push, pull or press to start it. Actually it's most awkward. I mean a dike that's not fully operational is a menace not a convenience! In spite of it all these people can turn round and build such things as the Spitfire! Yet they are content to go on living in their quaint old way. If I were English I would too no doubt. — Thank Goodness. I'm not that's all. All the things that I was taught when I was a kid I use now to guide me. I am never in doubt as to what I think is right or wrong. For this I am thankful. I have learnt many lessons and now I find the experience gained invaluable.

Wednesday 20 October: I do another X-country. After T/O I climb to 2½ thous and Stratford on Avon which I reach dead on ETA without mishap nor panic. Here I turn for Fenbury in Wales, leaving Shakespeare's birthplace behind. About half way I run into heavy cloud and rain, and am down to about 1400 ft. I reach Fenbury and have a little clear weather. It is a beautiful little township. I s/c from here for Little Rissington and get into more rain. I fly at about 1200 ft and clear hilltops by about 150 to 200 ft but I have spot heights on my maps and am on track. At Little Rissington I land on their SW-NE uphill downhill runway and report to the duty pilot while the crate is refuelled. He will not allow me to t/o again due to the weather and I'm as mad as hell. However after I have a lousy lunch in a rotten mess, he lets me go — I think I talk him into it. I check in at Met section — gear up, and scramble. Little Rissington is a Wimp OTU for Coastal, (Wimps being all white). I see a couple of Tomahawks, Martinettes and Spits hanging around though. I s/c Rushden without delay and get a little off track due to a wind change, but correct near Northampton and arrive over Rushden on time. Nearby is a huge Fort drome and soon after I s/c base I land up amongst about 96 of them evidently beginning a raid. I slip in on one at about 30 yds. He turns his guns on me so I freeze. Soon a Mosquito IV shoots me up, followed by a Beauie. I am a little cheesed and follow suit by scaring hell out of some poor cow in a Tiger. I should hate to think it was his first solo! I finally arrive at base all in order — a really good trip.

Thursday 21 October: One raider bagged last night.

Some Italian prisoners (17 of 'em) are digging potatoes near our dispersal. Tom and I go across. They are both amusing and interesting to talk to. There are three ex-pilots amongst them, (Macchis) shot down by Spits and 40s over El Alemein. Others were captured by Aussies at Derna, Benghazi and Sollum. They had no time for Australians for on capture they were deprived of watches, rings, cigarettes, money, shirts — in fact anything of value! Some seem very decent clean quiet intelligent chaps.

Tuesday 26 October: Tom, Allan Stutter and I leave by tender for Bramcote at 1330 hours. On the way we have the WAAF driver stop at the 'Brown Cow' where we have a couple or six. I find the 25-odd mile drive most interesting.

Bramcote, 105 OTU Wimpies for Transport Command is a large station, and our quarters are very decent, being centrally heated throughout. The Mess is wonderful and in general I think I am going to like the place very much — the lights and milds are extra! The BAT course is to last a week.

Sunday 31 October: How disillusioned I was! The beam is not going too well. I have never been so browned off with my flying as now. Our course is extended another week which makes things more dim. I attribute a lot of my lack of success to my instructor, a limey named Topley (F/Sgt) I hate his hide. Even writing his name irritates me.

Here I have found my long-thought opinion that English ground staff, except those working directly on aircraft, are a poor mob even more strongly borne out. Their name chair-crew is most appropriate. They have a superior, even scornful attitude towards all aircrew. Personally I lay it down to jealousy. It is not a nice thing to see at all, after all who is it who lose their lives in the RAF? Certainly not those who stay back at home while the boys go over night after night, day after day. Those boys are doing a fine job, risking all they have while they're about it. Should not they then be given the privileges and should they not be looked up to and respected? I certainly admire anyone who is, or has been, on ops.

We have been ejected from the Mess to a Mess of our own — Aircrew Mess they call it but here we are all happy pilots, wops, ags, navs, bombs etc. for there's not a ground staff Joe around and we forget them, and all to do with the RAF.

Wednesday 3 November: One bandit destroyed last night, two the night before and one the night before that, all south east from here. Still very sick of the beam although I want very much to set it all up, because the ability to execute a SBA is a very valuable asset to a pilot. This fact makes me more angry than ever. With a good <u>quiet</u> instructor I am sure that I would find as little difficulty with this type of flying as I have found with any other.

The arrival of a couple of Airgraphs from home improve the day a lot. Still no word from Pat, and this shakes me. I find I am easily annoyed now which I know is strange, still I have not come to showing it outwardly yet. I am also not hungry and get very tired. I think I must have one foot in the grave!

Friday 5 November: Topley, Tom and I go on a beam hop. We go away up past Nottingham before a/c about 250. Near Derby we run into heavy cloud and ice, and lose height but the danger of balloons is rather grim. Topley says he can see one, but I see some dozens from 0 to 5 thou on the port side. I am not that worried if we hit any or not, so don't tell him till we are right on them. At 300 odd we pass Stoke-on-Trent and proceed to get lost near Crewe. It is very bumpy and we are now at about 800 ft. We pick up Pershore beam, and then our own, and home on the QDR of 095. We get home whole — interesting trip, it could have been!

We have a little time off now so we decide to go to London by train, Dave Hughes accompanies us. On the way down we decide to go on to Brighton. And so on arrival at Euston we go straight to Victoria by taxi and have just nice time for a cup of tea before our train. We just step onto the Brighton platform at about 6.30 in time to hear the alert go followed shortly by the pips. It is just dusk and there are a few low clouds, however I see them coming in, quite high, about 20. Flak in long crimson stabs goes up through the cloud. They are sending a grand lot up. We stop for a minute to watch and then carry on for we are in a hurry because we want to get back to London tonight after seeing a few friends. In any case they break up soon and taking very effective avoiding action go on towards the London area — somebody's going to get it.

We go to the Met, see a few cobbers, get the latest local gen, and clear out down to the 'Albion Mansions' where I can find nothing out about Pat's watch which makes me mad. I leave a note for Sec. Officers' Mess.

I leave Dave and Tom here and go to the Aggs where there is bags of panic and surprise. They insist on supper so I miss our prearranged train! We have a great old yarn and bingo a bottle of port. I am glad to see them all and hear their news. At London I am told two Jerries were downed — good show, but not enough. Having no idea where Tom and Dave are in this big black city I set out alone at 12.20 am after a taxi which is no mean feat in the London I know after midnight. However at about 1 o'clock I get one with two Canucks, and eventually get to Church Army Hostel, Seymour Place after considerable panic. Here I expect to find the others, but am wrong, so go to bed and forget it. I'll find 'em in daylight tomorrow.

Saturday 6 November: I go straight to the Boomerang Club for breakfast at 11.45 (and as I thought find Tom and Dave who had spent the night at the Lion Club). We have an excellent meal and after signing this and that, reading the pucka gen and cheesing to all we know, breeze down the strand shopping, and we certainly weave — Pat I need assistance! Actually I am doing the impossible because I am doing two things at once — shopping and also seeing a little of London. There are numerous craters and wrecked buildings still from the great Blitz? The area around St Paul's is I think the most wrecked and bent as far as I see. I spend a little while inside St Paul's, where I was not lost thanks to the knowledge of the place Hon's drawing gave me. I go straight to the things I want to see, the high altar, whispering gallery etc. It is certainly a fine piece of work. — Wren knew his onions. I also visit Westminster Abbey, but having little time on hand do not look about much for I shall return one day to make a job of it. I am not at all impressed by old Father Thames, he's such a battletorn old river now. In our travels I see No. 10 Downing St, White Hall, Buckingham Palace, Hyde Park, St James Park, Marble Arch, Trafalgar Square, Piccadilly Circus, Leicester Square and Berkeley Square. I am not bubbling with enthusiasm over London. I cannot help thinking as I see these famous old buildings — I don't know what I feel actually, perhaps it's history or simple dignity or an overpowering sense of permanence. At length we catch our train back to Rugby where we get a quick meal before the train to Nuneaton.

Recently Jerry has been sending over small numbers of 'sneak-raiders' — ME410s and JU188s, new, very fast German fighter-bombers. Last night some were over the London area. A couple of large HEs hit a dance hall. Very heavy casualties were reported — some 200 I believe. At the time two cinemas opposite were just coming out and crowds in the street received a number of smaller bombs and incendiaries amongst them. This is the first bombing incident that I have heard the people in the street talk of much. Several of the raiders were destroyed. Not much is known about either of these new A/C.

At 1730 Tom and I (Tom has had the beam too) clear out and train to Rugby. I go to Hobley's for a while before going to Lawford where I spend the night. I wish that I was back here for good. There are a couple of Airgraphs here for me from home and Snake — no sea mail from Pat.

Tuesday 9 November: I get up at 1200 for breakfast and then go into Rugby. Here, in a little jewellers, I buy Pat a bracelet made entirely from English 3d. pieces. I have been after one for some time. I meet a few of the boys in town and have a sundry jug.

This is the third week on the beam, (now extended another week), and I'm heartily sick of it all and Topley. I think he's one of the strangest pilots I have ever met — he can fly well though, it's just his rotten manner and nasty character. Going bad. Some evenings we spend in Nuneaton to get away from the beam for awhile. We make our own fun and do alright.

Sunday 14 November: Went to Nuneaton last night and had quite a bit of fun, but it is bitterly cold these nights and sometimes drizzling. The carnival is not bad, I can usually manage to win a cigar at the shooting gallery. The dance at the Co-op isn't bad either. Back at Bramcote we get our first snow for the season. Tom, coming from Queensland, is amazed so we rub it on his nose and put it in his bed. I have been told I shall return to Lawford tomorrow — boy! am I pleased Tom is going too. 29 hours on the beam.

Wednesday 17 November: Jerry again over in the early morning. There are many casualties and damage is considerable. (Will omit bombing incidents unless extraordinary in future — so frequent I'll fill the book!) I am to do a week's day flying now before I go to night flying. Am in B Flight with Tom. Two chaps are killed today. I have no idea what happened. I knew neither of them well. Quite a number have pranged here since I've been around. (Tom should have been the stooge!) I have not flown since my return from Bramcote visibility being almost zero, or else a heavy ground haze. It is extremely cold and damp always now. I have everything on and my shirt tucked over it.

Friday 19 November: It is very cold — think I'll go nuts soon! Have a couple of Airgraphs from home and a parcel from Ararat, which is just the bestest! Have not flown yet — weather very duff. A Spit II flopped in hopelessly lost. England, this England — what a dump.

Go to Hobley's after tea. Riding the bike home in the fog is fun, but cold! (I split my lip this morning playing rugby and this is as sore as hell.) Sent cables home, Ararat and to Pat.

Saturday 20 November: Get up for breakfast at about 1100 and go into Rugby. It is still as cold as charity. I buy an identity bracelet for one pound seven and six and also an electric fire for one pound seven and six — much to the amusement of the boys. Back at camp we try her out and she's a beaut — cooks toast like hell. I add about 19 ft of A/C flex. All the ponds and water holes about the place are constantly covered with ice. My fingers, toes and ears are always cold. Tom finds it very uncomfortable.

I think I have almost seen every A/C in the service over here now. The types that I had not seen before I think are: Mossie, Tiff, Wimpie, Lanc, Hali, Stirling, Bolt, Mustang, Maggie, Daffie, Botha, Albamarle, Blenheim, Whitly, Horsa, 109, 110, 111, 190, 217 Hampden, Whirli, Ensign, Flamingo, Harrow, Scion, Toma, Fulmar and several new types I cannot recognise. I have flown in a great many types myself. The fastest I have been is about 490 mph in a Mosquito II.

Everything in the garden is reasonably lovely since being away from Bat. I don't feel too bad about anything in particular. There are amongst the Aussies on this camp a few greasers — they're not bad blokes but they are rather loud mouthed and go the beer and women too much.

Monday 22 November: I fly for the first time since returning from Bramcote. I do an hour's low flying and have a hell of a lot of fun shooting up farms and Land Army girls working on hay stacks, also a Tiger Moth — the best bit of fun I've had in England in the air.

Am posted to Night-fighter flight — this'll be good!

We always have a fire in the hut now which keeps things above freezing point. My feet have been wet for the last week — hence I suppose the cold I now have. I write Pat a long letter by Air Mail, also some Airgraphs home.

Thursday 25 November: Yesterday I received some ship mail from Aussie.

This night work is a great lurk — much more operational. I feel quite at home. Old 'Indigo Jones' the Met bloke is wizard. We fly all night and sleep? all day. Five meals a day are easily worked. Last Tuesday night Berlin got a hell of a doing from heavies of Bomber Command. They lost 20 crates.

I have definite confirmation now that Cookie has Pat's watch. — I'm gunna toe that girl's rudder when I get home. I went to Bilton last night (night off). Had a regular weekly grog party. Good show, but you have to drink so much!

Friday 26 November: Last night was wizard for flying. I find the MKII airfield lighting extra good. Approaches are made easy by glide path indicators (4½° & 5½°) and runways, perimeter tracks taxi posts etc. are extremely elaborate. There is never an horizon in this country, I/F therefore must be up to scratch — this I must polish up. I won't prang, but I am not perfect yet. The whole affair is extremely complicated what with pundits, occults etc., but wizard. They <u>have</u> got N/F taped in this country.

Today I get a cable from Pat saying that the watch has arrived safely also the parcel Arthur took back with the Norwegian bracelet and RAF wings. I also get a wallet and <u>photo</u>. This is a regular bingo show. This has certainly taken a load off my mind. All I wish now is that the journey has not given the works a shaky do. It went perfectly for six day test in Taunton — so here's hoping. The parcel was a regular flap — I thought it would be from home. Disillusioned mug! I shall let her off the kick in the rudder I was saving up now. Jeez what a girl to leave in such a hell of a hurry — wait till we get home. Today is cold again with frost still thick at 1430. The radiator is wizard. Six of us sit in the bath for an hour and a half, singing hymns!

Total losses to dawn Nov 21st:

	Axis	Allies
A/C	18,328	12,439
Personnel	30,671	49,645

(Official AM Figures)

Airgraphs are arriving fairly frequently now, I look forward to them every day.

Today an erk tells me that the English weather has deteriorated a great deal since outbreak of war. He lays it down in all good faith and sincerity, to the war itself— to the fact that all the bullets, shells, aircraft etc. moving through the air 'have upset the spheres and atmosphere'. There is far too much optimism about the termination of the war soon in my opinion. People here take it almost for granted that it's all as good as finished and that we can relax a little. Far from it, now that we have perhaps the advantage we should put all we've got into it and work for a crippling blow. Lately the press have been throwing much about regarding this, there have also been some very pointed cartoons.

My N/F Instructor, Sgt Pryer, is a good bloke and we get on well together. This makes a great deal of difference. There is a new clumsy blundering Queenslander in our hut now, who thinks the sun shines out his ears. I for one cannot see it. One night is the same as the next — we fly. I shall have a night off with Tom tomorrow night. We plan to go to Leicester.

There was an extremely thick fog in London the other night (Saturday) causing untold panic. Buses had to be navigated by waving torches and streets were illuminated by newspapers dipped in oil and ignited. Jerry was over at the same time and caused damage and casualties.

Thursday 2 December: I am told we cannot travel more than 20 miles from our station during Xmas week! This is to let war workers take holidays in comparative comfort — at least whilst travelling. I take a misty view of it all because I am supposed to be going shooting and fishing in Scotland.

Jeez they're at us again! Today I collect two needles in the left arm and now they're beginning to work. Still we went into Rugby to the pictures. (Tom, Allan and myself.) A Tiff comes in today with a duff motor. I take a photo of it. I spend a dim night with a crook arm but as we are all the same way, the hut is very jovial.

Friday 3 December: Cold as hell with a damp heavy fog.

What I am to do with myself after the war still has me foxed, but I suppose I must wait until the hurdle becomes visible before jumping it. Here of course Pat comes into the question, or should I say the question revolves round her. Having met her I know my outlook has changed entirely. Had I not met her I may at this time have been doing things far different to what I am. I have not the slightest fear of death, rather perhaps have I learnt to scorn it, but now I find myself being extra careful and as it were, 'looking before I leap'. Life is a wonderful thing, this I have realized far more fully.

Went to Black Horse last night on night off. Navigated the bike into a graveyard by mistake. Arrived home with a phone and book, notices, signs, cups and the usual junk! An extremely amusing evening indeed. Ron Dent on the mat for not preparing his address to N/F. F today. He gets away with admonishment. I set a Verey YY off in the hut about 1.45 am with highly satisfactory results! Hill and valley fog. Pundits a little indistinct. Have to fly very low.

Thursday 9 December: The same old thing during the day as it is every day now. I am quite used to my life and surroundings here now and quite content. I enjoy the company of 'the Guild' very much and hope we all stick together in the future. All are Anzacs — the bolshiest mob ever to hit 8(P) AFU I'll bet — always in trouble, always in fun — always looking a rough and tumble lot! Last night and early this morning we smoked out huts 4 and 6 with Verey YYs. Had 'Spam' and toast for supper (4th) at 0315! Icing 4 thou. Fog.

Friday 10 December: Blow the PO up about my mail. Pay is a muck up. I see a great many Lancasters pass at 1000' steering 150° at perhaps 6 min intervals. Also Forts in 26s steering about 080° at 8 thou. Cloud 8/10ths. Vis. good, 10 miles. Very early this morning some snow fell. I awoke to find the ground quite white. Ice was forming on the inside of my A/C last night.

Ron and I have decided to put in for the East. We have had England, and the RAF <u>here</u>. Desert warfare sounds pretty good. We'll see a little more world too. Mosquito II in last night — U/S L/I light. Straight from factory.

Tuesday 14 December: I buy a new bike for eleven pounds from P/O Wallace, a Cunuck, and an extra good chap. Tom, Allan and I are going back to B Flight for a week. We are all to leave this station next week for good, and will go to Snitterfield to wait for our OTU postings. The 'Guild' are still together. Here we shall have 9 days leave.

Friday 17 December: A little mail turns up. Airgraphs from Jim Jordan and Joan Perry amongst them. Jim's news is very welcome, especially the trout gen. Joan tells me a good deal about Pat. Yesterday afternoon there was a bullo parade in earnest. We made a joke of it. Afterwards we went into Rugby to get over it. (Allan, Tom and myself.) Good time. Today is duff with wet heavy fog. I spend my time bludging. After tea we go to Rugby again. We go to 'Coney Island' with Betty Grable — good show, but she looks a lot different to herself in reality. I saw her at the Astor Roof Garden on Broadway. Coming out a cat causes panic during a call on it by nature. At the YMCA Tom's light is stolen.

Some of these English people have got guts, they have feeling, they have what it takes. England is unbeatable. She has a magnificent spirit — but I live in Aussie. Two dozen bottles of beer arrive to our hut, but we are taken in — it's daft! Crewing up is simplified by finding chaps from your home town or district. (It also makes it easier for the Old Man — all the coffins arrive on the same train!) There is a prang tonight but nobody killed — a crate goes for a burton about 5 miles away from the drome. I don't know where they belonged. There's a Kiwi amongst them.

Saturday 18 December: There is heavy wet fog today and we cannot leave the ground.

At about 1640 hours Tom, Allan and I bike to Rugby and catch the train to Leicester. On arrival we try for accommodation at the celebrated Belle Hotel. Finally after some trying we get into the Grand, a very nice old place and quite high class.

Sunday 19 December: Get up at 1030 hours and we go for a walk all about town looking the place over. I am amazed by the place. It is all very modern and clean and far more like home than any other place I have yet seen in England. It is certainly nice to see it all. Before dinner we drink a few whiskies with some 8th USAAF Fort aircrew. They aren't bad chaps either, we get their whisky for them for they <u>can't</u> buy them!

(Here I learn that during the Russo-Finland conflict, great numbers of

British troops were ready for embarkation to Finland <u>on board their ships</u>. Great numbers of warships were also ready with them! Hmm!!) At length after visiting the Swan with Two Necks we catch our train back to Rugby. Tom is a sad case, but Allan and I are 100%. We have a lot of trouble with Tom, and have to take turns in dinking him home — a dead weight, quite lifeless. He's bad. I shall certainly visit Leicester again soon. This has been the best little bash that I have had in England.

Monday 20 December: Get a mysterious letter from Pat, written 9/9/43. It has on it, 'found on road and posted in this condition at n'down — P.M.'

Friday 24 December: Allan and I go to Leicester on the 7.35 pm train from Rugby straight after pancaking from a X-country (Base–Usk–High Wycombe–Thropston–Lutterworth–Base.) It was a wizard trip. I was first pilot, Allan 2nd. Sims was Nav. The Welsh countryside is beautiful from the air. We found Usk and HW covered completely with low cloud. Just before arrival at Lutterworth visibility dropped to almost nil. (We made two starts, the first A/C I put U/S because of failure of starboard motor.)

We stay at the Grand again (Room 95). Just manage to get into Palais. The night is quite eventful as any Xmas Eve is and I have a good time but not as good as many I have had in the past. I lend Allan ten pounds, this is one way to save money.

Saturday 25 December: XMAS DAY! I have a good breakfast at 1000 (with sugar). We are talked into staying for Xmas Dinner which, after a visit to Les, the nearby proprietor, where we meet dozens of people, I enjoy very much. This is the first taste of chicken I have had since arrival in England. We spend the afternoon very pleasantly and after afternoon tea we check out of the Grand. Eventually we catch our train and return to camp at about 11.30 after having spent a very quiet but enjoyable time, but only just. On arrival back here we find the Mess almost upside down about an inch deep in beer. I am told it has been so for 36 hours. I grab some mail but cannot read it (Pat has taken to Airgraphs, the little beaut).

We join in the do, and soon I'm really happy. I find Greenbottle quite well lit up. Sgt Pryce buys me a few — dear old Prycie, I like this Englishman. Steinstreet and Scragg are 'out'. Tom and I turn on a dancing act and sing 'Waltzing Matilda'. F/Lt Kearsey, the Battle of Britain boy is a fine type in a fine mood. They tell me he's been this way for a day and a half. I've never seen so many happy persons all together like this before in my life — it's great. What a beer up, there's ACFAs, ACWs, S/Ls, P/Os, Sgts, F/Lts, civies ATS — all are here together.

Sunday 26 December: Now here's the thick end of the raw prawn! — some greaser has pinched my eleven pound bike during the night — this I find out when eventually I get around to getting up at lunch time (I was supposed to fly this morning!) By Jeez I'm wild. I wonder shall I ever see it again, it was a wizard bike, I inform the SPs. This has been a good Xmas, even though a long way from home. I have received recent and good news from both home and Pat. I hope I shall be home for the next — surely there is no sweeter word than this. I am all disorganised tonight and cannot find a thing. Damn.

Tuesday 28 December: Last night at 8 a 'Boxing Day Social Evening' began. It turned out to be another regular 'animal act'. Greenie was there, and the Guild soon settled down to solid soaking. Pryce almost got his own back on me. I helped Mac a bit to regain life once. The turkey, pork and ham we thieved from inside was wizard. It was a farewell party for the Guild and what a do. Tom ground looped early in the show so Greenie and I put him to bed. He was ill, but not bad. Ron, Snow and I fry our 6 eggs in marg. in an old tin lid. They were extra and brought me back to normal. It was hard, but necessary, to get up this morning. We begin getting cleared and all fixed up to leave. I eat 4 aspirins at a time for I feel a little duff.

Wednesday 29 December: At length after bags of panic we leave Church Lawford and train from Dunchurch to Leamington Spa where we eat and change trains. We have a hell of a lot of flap, but at length arrive here at Snitterfield. Nobody receives us, so the Guild take over and thieve their way into a good hut all together (Right now the place looks quite Guildish). We scramble, some to the Golden Cross down the road, and some to a little cafe (this is for me). Everything is okay. There seems to be oodles of women and good little pubs about. Snow came home from the GC — as happy as a lizard — he's met a WAAF (Sylvia) and has all the gen about the place.

Friday 31 December: Here's the leave we've been waiting for. After a hell of a lot of bother we leave at about 4 pm. The Guild is splitting, but Allan, Snow and I go as far as London together arriving there at about 11.15. It is New Year's Eve and we do not have a single drink! Everyone but us seems to be tight. I'm off to Scotland as set up by Arthur Plant before he left for home.

The trip to London is uneventful. I sleep. I go from Victoria to Euston by tube, and I am sure that but for the assistance of a very nice old gentleman, I should have become horribly foxed. (I think he was a clergyman.) At

Euston a typical RAF SP mug tells me that I shan't get a connection at Carlyle for the St Bosells train on a Sunday morning. I grin at him and board the train, secretly dubious. Here I have a mixed selection of persons — a Yank Fort navigator, several erks, a Scotch infantryman and English Tommy.

Sunday 2 January 1944: Somewhere around Crewe the morning finds us. The train is very hot inside. It is bright moonlight. The curtains go up. More spam and apples. Round about 6.15 am I stagger off at Carlyle and have a hot cup of tea. I find the Scotch talk most amusing indeed at first. I catch the train that supposedly wasn't, to St Boswells after about half an hour's wait. At. St B I am just about to flop out of the carriage when the train begins. I quietly ask a Scotsman (army) to open the door for me to bale out. He panics a lot and jibbers away in Scotch about the train going too fast and another stop about an hour up the line — horrible specimen. And so I miss out at St B! At Melrose I pile out, and, as luck (nothing else) would have it, I find a taxi and go to Ancrum pronto. The wee Scot has never heard of 'Woodside' and stings me one pound for the ride to Ancrum. At the PO I am most welcome for, as they have not yet recovered from New Year celebrations, the telegram I sent is still undelivered. I go with the bloke in the car to deliver myself and the wire.

On sight I like Tom Maclean a heavily-built blue eyed, jovial Scotsman. Euph too I like very much and at once I know that I am going to be happy here. After studying several old guns I have a meal — bacon, eggs, home made scones, butter and jam etc. Jeez this is good. After this I feel very tired and so sleep until 4.30 pm when I again eat like a king. We spend the night talking a great deal, for there is plenty to chat about, and after another meal I turn in. I am very tired having not slept much for two nights running.

Monday 3 January: I arise at about noon and eat, after which Euph takes me down to see the old home of the Lord and Lady, now a hospital, and along the river a little and up the glen home again. I am very interested in it all. Here is real tradition. The trees about the home must be very old. The house itself is not beautiful nor extraordinary, but perhaps just big. It has been added to and added to by its different inhabitants away down the line. The rest of the walk is very pretty and I enjoy it a lot. Tom has been away shooting all day and at tea returns full of vim and humour with his huge Labrador retriever, Biddy. Again we spend the evening around the fire. I am very happy and at home. I like the look of this Scotland.

Tuesday 4 January: Up early and, of course, eggs and bacon for breakfast again. Tom gives me a gun and ammunition enough to stop an invasion and with Peter and Biddy we give the duck on the Teviot a pasting. Peter retrieves for me. We have a good morning and some rabbits are added to the bag. After dinner we do some shooting over open burrows with ferrets and have great fun. I'm not so out of touch with the gun as I thought I would be. This is just the sort of leave I need — away from A/C (although Beaus and Hurricanes are constantly overhead). After tea I write home and to Pat. The kitten Tousie and I are good friends now, tho' still I hate cats. The wee pouvie Wendy too is very friendly.

Wednesday 5 January: Peter and I go up on the hill. There are plenty rabbits moving, but the fog is too heavy for decent shooting. After dinner we tour the farms on the Estate, which is 23,000 acres in area, to pay the rabbitmen. I see Jedburgh just for a moment, a small old historic tweed and hosiery manufacturing town with a fine old Abbey and Castle, built on the banks of the Jed. I am greatly interested in the scenery, the people I see, the farms, indeed everything — who wouldn't be? It is dark when we get home. We soon have the fires going and tea on the table and jeez I fill up. Food like this is wonderful. I have an idea what it will be like to go home again now.

Thursday 6 January: Today is the big day. Eight shooters from Newcastle come up. They invite me to shoot with them, a high honour I believe. We give the ducks, pheasants, partridges, rabbits and crows a go in the morning in the afternoon rabbits, badgers, crows, foxes, pheasants, partridges and wood-pigeons. This is the real 'old country' shooting. We have beaters. When a bird comes over they call 'Pigeon over, Sir!' for instance. Of course this is wizard to me. I have a hell of a good day. We all have tea together and I am invited by one chap to spend a leave at his place. I hope I can. (A Mr Fail) Later I eat a whole roast rabbit and half a pheasant! This is after we visit 'Frankies' in Denham.

Friday 7 January: Today Tom and I batch because Euph goes to Hawick to do Red Cross work. We shoot the crows in the back wood first with all eleven dogs. We spend a lot of time unsuccessfully trying to find a cock pheasant that I wounded. After lunch we shoot over open burrows on the riverside and get 23 pairs. I almost catch a deer that becomes caught in heavy driftwood. I find the animals such as the mole, weasel, badger and squirrel which are new to me very interesting, also the strange bird-life.

Saturday 8 January: The time has passed so quickly and I do not feel at all like returning, however tomorrow it must be.

I take three of the dogs up to the back wood and get a couple of pair quite easily in the morning. Today we have the first drop of rain since I arrived, and even then it is very fine. The nights have been clear and cold, the days fine but with little sunshine. After dinner we go to Jedburgh in the car. I buy some postcards (after Tom and I have a couple in the Spread Eagle). I also take the chance to have a look round the place and to send a cable home and to Pat. We meet Nurse Ann Wilson and take her back for tea. It is almost dark when we have finished but I sneak up the back for a shot. I don't get it except for a clout at a crow. We go down to see 'Tommie the Jew' in Ancrum and also the PO people (unfortunately they are going out). We call in at the hospital on the way home and see the nurses and have tea. At midnight we have supper at home and I go to bed at about 0140 hours.

Sunday 9 January: Ann and I climb the hill to the old tower in the morning, built in 1835. There are 228 steps and at the top the view is magnificent. I collect two pigeon eggs, they are early nesting surely? I have the gun but see nothing. In the afternoon I pack up, have a bath, and after tea and a long chat by the fire they run me to the Hawick bus in the car. It is with great sorrow that I leave Tom and Euph. They are wonderful persons, each of them, and they have given me a wonderful time making me feel as much at home as possible. I like Scotland a great deal more than England. Some day perhaps I can return to see it. The mountains and the woods, the burns and the glens, the hills and the heather. It is the people too so quaint yet so kind and understanding. And so I go by bus to Hawick where, until my train leaves at 11.30, I pass the time in the YM.

I can't get a word in edgeways for people asking me about Aussie! This cheeses me. Next the chip shop runs out just as I arrive, then the train is late, then it is full and I must stand. I arrive at Carlyle thoroughly cheesed. At Crewe I change and still no seat! At Nuneaton I get out to go to Leamington but retrain because I can't, and alight at Rugby to wait 1½ hours for the Leamington train. I poke about Leamington. Eventually I land in camp 7 hours AWL.

The first shock is that Snow, Ron and Norm are posted to 11OTU Westcott. They leave tomorrow. Good luck to 'em! (Wimpies.)

Next a letter from Pat — and also RAAF HQ. Pat's letter shakes me she reckons she's changed! — blonde streak or some'm and darker. I shall write to her tonight!

Wednesday 12 January: An Aussie (Heins) was killed the other night when he flew into the Rugby radio masts. They stand some 1180 ft above sea level (about 900 ft above C.L. drome). He must have been asking for it, he would know very well that they were there. This chicken shan't go that way.

Friday 14 January: I go to Leamington (went to Stratford-on-Avon yesterday afternoon — quaint old place, very historic and full of interest. The shops were closed for a 'half day'. I found a small cafe where I sat a long time taking in its oldness).

In Leamington I first have lunch before doing a little shopping. In the afternoon I go to the pictures. I catch a train about 6 back to Bearley where I get my bike and go in search of the Olde Bull Inn. This I find to be the nicest little place of its kind in England that I have yet visited. It was first erected in the 13th century and of course has since been renovated, but is still very old, genuinely old, and interesting. The atmosphere is far above the standard of the usual English 'pub'. Here I have a wizard meal of two eggs, cutlets, sausage, chips, and bacon followed by cream trifle, cheese, biscuits and butter. Coffee is served in the lounge (with real sugar). The standard of people is much higher too than the usual 'pub type'. I have a very pleasant evening chatting, with an odd nip, and leave about 10 pm. This is the sort of English place I should like Pat to see.

Wednesday 19 January: Today is an awful day. It never stops raining. Cold, wet and miserable, in true Royal Air Force fashion, they decide to collect some wood for the Mess. I get as wet as a shag and as cheesed off as hell. Flying is impossible all day.

To the collector of taxes:

'Dear Sir,
For the following reasons I am unable to meet your demand note for Income Tax.

I have been bombed, blasted, burnt and sandbagged, walked on, set upon, helped up, held down, flattened out and squeezed out by Income Tax, Super Tax, Tobacco Tax, Purchase Tax, Beer Tax, Amusements Tax, Spirit Tax, Motor Tax and every Society, Organisation and Club, that the inventive mind of man can conceive, to extract what I may or may not have in my possession, for the Red Cross, Black Cross, Double Cross and every bloody cross and Hospital in town and country.

The Government has governed my business until I do not know who the hell owns it. I am suspected, inspected, examined, informed, required and commanded so that I do not know who I am, what I am or why I am here at all.

All I know is that I am supposed to have an inexhaustible amount of money for every need, desire or hope of the human race, and because I shall not go out and beg, borrow or steal money to give away, I am ousted, boycotted, talked about, talked to, lied to, lied about, held up, held down, robbed and damned near ruined.

The only reason I am still clinging to life at all is to see what the bloody hell is going to happen next.

Yours faithfully
Etc.'

Thursday 20 January: I fly a S/L to Bramcote and come back by myself. Visibility is particularly bad so I avoid the Coventry area and come home via Lawford.

At about 4.30 I organise and set-off for London. At Leamington Spa I catch a fast London train and get into only a moderately interesting compartment and consequently the trip is not too brilliant. At Paddington I dodge the SPs and go straight to the Strand Palace. At about 9.30 the alert goes and soon Jerry is overhead good and proper. The roar of the guns is terrific. I go out the back to watch. There is fine cloud at about 3,500 ft and the searchlights, very great in number, have difficulty in penetrating well enough to light an A/C up well. There seem to be a number of bandits, at one time there are about 5 overhead. I see a fire already towards inner London. Last night the RAF dropped 2,300 tons on Berlin (about 1000 A/C operating, losing 33. This must be a reprisal.)

A bomb shrieks down about a mile away and that even shakes the place. Five flares are dropped at East Finchley Station, but they do not bomb across them. The barrage of flak going up is terrific. I can see Z-flak (new) going up also. Shrapnel falls around me giving me the creeps. This stuff perhaps 6 inches long and ½ to ¾" square whizzes down at great velocity and makes a wicked noise. A great many people have been killed by it. At about 10 he seems to have had it and moves NE.

At about 3.45 Jerry comes again. I thought he would. The cloud is down to some 400–500 ft and Jerry himself cannot be more than 800 ft Searchlights and flak are all over the place. I soon get to sleep again hoping nothing blows me clean out of bed.

Saturday 22 January: At breakfast I learn that the raid was the largest since the Blitz days, 90 odd A/C being used. They claim 10 definitely destroyed. There was considerable damage and casualties. NB 28th January — 14 A/C were officially destroyed, it has now been announced.

About 11.30 am I leave to catch my train at Paddington. I meet a number of people in the tube, but none are going quite 'my way'! I catch the fast 6.10 to Leamington Spa stopping Bicester, Banbury and Leamington. The compartment is quite bright. There is a very jovial Welshman, full of talk and fun. Also a Tommy, an Erk, a civi bloke and woman. At Leamington I get out just in time to catch the train to Bearley where I collect my bike, have a snack at the cafe and cycle to the airfield.

I have suddenly found myself settling down in England quite well. I have oodles of moans, but I am always discovering something new in interest or beauty — or even quaintness. It is the people just so much better off than the man in the street that I like best, both those at the top and those at the bottom I dislike, the middle man I don't mind, but between 'middle and top', I fit in well.

Monday 24 January: Get weaving in the air again. I do two trips today. The second trip I do in very duff weather. I get a parcel from the Ararat folk containing peaches, Xmas pudding, chocolate etc. I appreciate these parcels very much when they come. I wish I could send something back again to sort of even things up instead of simply a cable.

'Ginger' Snelling and I cycle to the Bull at about 8 pm, where we have the usual good time: The wind is very strong, almost a gale.

Wednesday 26 January: I do some NFTs all day. The weather is duff and only for 'Smokey Joe' I should have been lost on two trips. The QBB is 5 to 800 and I lose a starboard motor on the runway just at lunchtime. Late in the afternoon the Aussies about the place put on a show taxying 6 crates around to dispersal. Jeez do we travel!, and we keep one crate running to bring us all back in — jigger walking it.

I visit the Bull after tea and have the usual good time. I have little difficulty in organising for Saturday night. The people here (Mr & Mrs Ralph Edwards) are very nice indeed and I get on very well with them. Mr Edwards is to take me to the Green Dragon one evening.

Saturday 29 January: I received a Xmas Box from the Aust. Comforts Fund containing an extremely acceptable assortment of foodstuffs and useful articles and materials — also the address of the packer(ess?): Miss Barbara Palliser, 36 Downes Avenue, North Brighton, Melbourne. I must write her a note soon, I'm sure a word or two received from those who receive their work, would not be amiss.

At about 2000 hrs Ginger and I set off to the Bull, and here I celebrate my 21st quite quietly — a good meal, a few drinks and a long chat before at about 2350 we set off home. I have an invitation to a nearby farm on

Monday night — I'll be there! I buy some Potato Crisps before leaving and these I eat at home in bed. By and large, I have a really good evening.

Sunday 30 January: I do three trips today. Nearly killed my dumb self when I stalled a crate at 1500 with flap and u/c down. Shook one for a while — recovery from a spin in these things is impossible and it is almost as impossible to bale out!

Tuesday 1 February: NFTs all day. After tea I go down to Jack Potter's place near Henley on Arden, named 'Beech Hill', where I meet a crowd of people and the two Land Girls on the place. We have a good night and at about 1.45 am I leave in the pouring rain to ride the 4 miles back to the drome. I am as wet and tired as a shag when I get home but I have had a good night nevertheless.

Saturday 5 February: Posted to 17 OTU Silverstone with a few of the old Deni boys. This looks like it. I've had it so shall do my best as a bomber captain to put up a good show. I want a 'Pommie' nav and wop, and the rest Aussies, definitely no Canadians.

Wednesday 9 February: Arrived at 17 OTU Silverstone, last night and have spent most of the time organising myself and studying 'types' for the crew. The game's on now in no uncertain fashion. The station is good and the food very good — an orange a day and milk to drink.

I left my Ronson lighter, which I got on 'USS Mount Vernon', back at Snitterfield. I hope I get it back again. I have written to the CMC. It seems we stay here for two weeks on ground school and crew up before going to the satellite for four weeks. We then return here to finish up. The crates are 3s on circuits and the rest 10s, so this is something. I am quite confident that all will work out okay eventually.

The bikes arrive eventually today which is a good show. I write to Pat.

Saturday 12 February: Things are going quite well in general. I have a complete crew — all Australian except for the bomb aimer who is an Englishman from Birmingham. The navigator, Des Murray comes from Queensland and is a very quiet and nice fellow, very keen and a gen man. The Wopag, Jock Gardner, comes from Melbourne; rear gunner from Launceston, Tas. and mid-upper from Melb. They are Geoff Allen and Bill Jackman respectively. The bomb aimer is named Ron Mayall, or Darkie. We get on well together and I am sure that things will go off well. The Wimp has many complications which we all must master. The cockpit drill, fuel and oil systems are particularly intricate. I had mail from home and Pat two days ago, which as usual made the day wonderful, especially Pat's mail (4 airgraphs and a letter by Air Mail).

A few nights ago O-Oboe returned from a 'nickle raid'. Before the engines had stopped the bomb aimer climbed out and walked into the port airscrew — his head went clean into the port side of the nose! Bad luck really, but this would not have happened if orders had been obeyed, and the Captain done his job correctly. Nav (Des) and I bike to the White Horse about 8 o'clock and spend a quiet evening talking. I like him a great deal and he is very keen. He did 13 hours at Narromine before being scrubbed. He is going to get me a couple of films for the camera — good show! It has been intensely cold these last few days although no rain has fallen. Surely it will get warmer soon.

Saturday 19 February: A letter today from Pat written in November! Jeez! what have they been doing with it? There are some photos which make it an extra good surprise.

The whole crew seem to have settled down now and we all know each other well. During the past week we have all been doing a great deal. Snow has been falling today and all day yesterday it fell steadily. The ground is very pretty clothed in a soft white carpet, but by hell it's cold at times.

Today I attended a 'gen lecture' by a W/C Cheddle on tactics, Jerry night fighter organisation and the secret weapons of ours and the enemy's. I must carry it all, as well as many other things that I should like to put in here, in my nut! It was a very good show — concentrated gen.

Monday 21 February: On Saturday night the target was Leipzig. Lancs and Halys were the main force — lost 79. The night before 2,500 tons went to Berlin. Last night the main target was Stuttgart 687 heavies went out and 606 came home. These losses are big compared with the usual. Something is a little amiss. Jerry too has been active in another direction — London. Last night he staged a fire raid and also the night before, dropping oil, fire, phosphorous and incendiaries as well as HEs. Considerable damage and casualties were reported even when only 73 bandits reached the London area on Saturday night. Last night Jerry was using 'window' — cheeky cow!

I am well in with the blokes in the photographic section of this place now — good show. I must see what I can do about my watch at the instrument section.

Thursday 24 February: We leave here today for the satellite at Turweston where I shall do a month's basic flying. Des will come across to join us in about 10 days time. Johnny Middleton and I bike our way across in the early afternoon. It is a really beautiful day, clear and sunny and so enjoyable after the cold weather and all the snow we have been having lately. All the crew sleep in the one hut, which is a good show. There seems to be a possibility of 36 hours leave tomorrow with luck, if so I think I'll whip down to Brighton. London has had comparatively heavy raids for the past five successive nights. On Tuesday night about 175 came across; 100 odd reaching the London area. Only 10 were shot down. This percentage is the same as we lose almost nightly and it isn't a bad effort on the part of the Luftwaffe. I should say 30 shot down was more reasonable but not even then really the shot. These attacks are the greatest since the Blitz days. I don't like it myself — a thoroughly bad show in fact.

Bill Jackman, one of my gunners, I find a very decent chap. I didn't know him so to speak until tonight, but I am more sure now than ever that he is a 'good man'. Des, Darkie, Jock and Geoff are 'good men' — she's a bang on crew I reckon, and it's up to me now to be a bang on Captain.

My bike goes for a walk tonight. I only hope somebody has simply borrowed it for the night and not permanently — gives me a rush.

Friday 25 February: Sure enough after breakfast I discover a Pommie with my mangle — 'thought it was somebody else!' After lunch Rod, Peter, a gunner Small and myself taxi to Brackley and get the London train. Here I taxi to Brighton train at Victoria, and finally get to Brighton at about 6.20. Jerry dropped some stuff over towards Whitehall on Wednesday night. I saw evidence near Euston in London, of the recent raids. They tell me the Treasury and Westminister were hit a bit. Jerry doesn't come over tonight anyway and I end up in bed finally at about 2.30 am.

Saturday 26 February: It is a dull day but there are a few Typhoon bombers overhead. At about 2.30 I catch the 3.8 to London where I taxi to the Boomerang Club to meet Peter and Rod for tea (which as usual is wizard). One of the famous London pea-soup fogs is just closing down and vision is already limited to about 75 yds and all the lights are on. It is quite a brown, yellowy colour.

We taxi to Marlybone Station, catch the 6.9 to Brackley and taxi to the airfield. I have a bit of a sore throat and am glad to get home. I heat a can of sweet corn on my radiator and write an Air Letter to Pat. I must try to write a lot of letters in the next few days, I am a long way behind, but not due to my own neglect for work has been stiff lately.

Thursday 2 March: Do a trip in a Wimp — most amazing to begin with. It's a case of PYFO all the time. This sums it up entirely. It certainly takes it out of you. I receive a parcel of shortbread from Pat; a cake and box of canned stuff from home — good show. After tea I go down to Syresham, a small village about 1½ miles away. There are two pubs here, The King's Head and The Belle Inn. This is the second time that I have been here. Tonight I go to the latter, and have quite a good time.

Sunday 5 March: I take the whole crew around the circuit (apart from Des.) Good show! Jeez they're dirty great heavy damned things, but I reckon I can manage them for another 80 hours or so!

I get two wizard letters from Pat; her mail is most interesting. She reckons that she can now understand why I don't like the idea of girls (like her) going into the Services. I am certainly glad of this, I knew she'd see what I meant — how much more so if she had come across here with us through America. How it all opens your eyes.

Monday 6 March: A parcel of assorted dried fruits and nuts comes from Pat. It's too hard for me to try to explain wonderful is not half a good enough word. After each day now I find myself pretty tired and worn out. Bed is a hard place to leave in the mornings. I do a little bombing today myself as B/A — bags of fun! The second bomb I land dead in the centre of the target, O error! (The first is about a 1000 yard error, hem!!) Am chewing a few of Pat's dried fruits while writing this — wizard. Time for bed now. Sore eyes. Weather poor early today improving later with lifting QBB. The boys set off for Germany about 7.30, quite a big force. Bed now.

Saturday 11 March: Bill Watson in King and our gang in Roger go for a stooge across to the Wash and back in formation. It's a pretty rough trip with a lot of low cloud. Afterwards I whip up to Lawford and then do a few dummy runs.

After tea all the crew except rear gunner go down to Buckingham per bike (in Bucks). We go to the White Heart first and then to the local hop. Buckingham is a nice sized little village old in architecture and layout, and would be very interesting if one had time enough to wander around. The other villages nearby the camp are a lot smaller except Beachley. Whitfield I like very much, built on the side of a hill with a small stream at the bottom over which a quaint old rustic bridge crosses. The houses are old with thatched roofs — not all, some are slate roofed. The road twists through the cottages and is very narrow. There is the usual little village green and square and an abundance of big friendly trees. Trees make such a difference. Whitfield is a green and fresh little place. Syresham is not half as pretty or interesting as Whitfield. Westbury is also a nice little place, perhaps a little more on the quaint side.

The dance is some show for everyone is merry. Des, Bill and I go through unhooked but Jock is diddled by the LA and gets back to camp around 0200. On the way down we pass down a particularly beautiful little stretch of country lane. On both sides there are hedges. It is just sunset. The evenings are getting longer now. There is a farm on the left with old broken buildings and disused farm equipment. There is an old bent elm leaning across the road. This would be lovely in Summer.

Monday 13 March: Bags of fun this morning — we do some dinghy drill in the Baths at Northampton. First crew in, and last out! High level bombing at night from 11,000. Results converted to 20,000 are 235. It is a very bad night with about 20° drift so this isn't too bad for mugs!

I do gunnery exercise. Darkie's map reading is very good. The Martinette does some bang on attacks for the boys. London was raided again last night and at least 13 were shot down. Mostly incendiaries were dropped.

Around our hut there are many elm trees and the crows are building in most of them. This surely is a sign of spring — thank goodness. I'm looking forward to seeing England in the springtime.

Thursday 16 March: Tonight is not very brilliant at all yet we fly. We have quite a hair-raising time and I am quite glad to get down again. It is around 1245 when we are waiting for the bus at our dispersal. An aircraft comes over and overshoots. As I watch it pass by at some 200 ft I sort of wonder somehow just how things are inside and who is in it, feeling happier still inside me to be down again. The bus arrives and I take my eyes off it to pick up my things. Suddenly the note of the engines changes and I am just in time unfortunately to pick up the nav lights as the A/C dives vertically into the ground near Beachley with full motor, and explodes with vivid scarlet flames. I am somewhat stunned because amidst the few blurred comments I hear, someone say, 'that's 352'. I remember that Peter took 352 K-King. The ammunition is now exploding the sky is brightly lit and black smoke comes away from the awful sight on the hill near Beachley. I think first, I thought of Pat, Peter's girl back in Australia. Then I thought of the crew — 'Moose', and the B/A, an Englishman. He always used to be mending bikes, funny sort of chap. P/O Dennis the other pilot. He'd just received the DFM. Small, the rear gunner, I wonder if he'd get out. Surely not, not out of this blaze. My mind is blank as I get into the bus. I light a cigarette. Nobody talks. We all knew Peter very well. We were in the Crew Room with him before take-off. I try not to look out on the way back, but somehow I must. The sky is still an orange colour. The ambulance goes past us —

not much need for that, I think. I feel a little upset inside — quite natural I suppose. I try to think what could have happened. Only one thing I'm sure. He must have raised his flaps in one go. Horrible business. We have supper, not that I feel like it, and go to bed. Somehow I go to sleep.

Friday 17 March: I get down to the Flight at about 1.30 pm to find that another crate has gone in, this time a ditching. All have got out, I am told, except the WOP, an English chap (also from our hut). They were picked up in the Wash by a destroyer. Thank God some are safe. Small, the rear gunner, in last night's prang has got out. He is very badly injured and burnt, but will probably live poor devil. I think it would have been better if he had gone too. All the rest went over. There will be no funeral as there is nothing to bury. I am learning to be more than careful. I am learning to trust nothing or nobody until I have checked things myself. I want to come out of this rotten business alive, if not, then due to enemy action, not my own.

Tuesday 21 March: Today the weather is duff due to a large cold front moving across. We shan't fly tonight I expect. I shall write home and to Pat. Time has been so short lately, I have not had time to write all that I should like. I receive news that Red Macdonald was eaten by sharks when he ditched his P-40 in SWP some place. Another crate went in last night, but not one of ours. It burnt right out. Things are a little grim at the moment!

Sunday 26 March: Last night all of us except Nav went down to Westbury where we had a very good time at the Reindeer Inn. Jock and Junior were most amusing on the way home. They found bike-riding most difficult. Today we move back to Silverstone where our long trips will commence. We shall only be four weeks there so this isn't too bad. After that I expect to go on some decent leave. It is a really lovely day today. I must admit this, even to Englishmen around me. The sun is clear in a very blue sky, the trees are budding; the grass is green and the birds are very happy. There are little grey squirrels about today too, little shy but inquisitive things which seem continuously jumping and twitching all over, very pretty.

Wednesday 29 March: I receive a letter from Pat, including some good photographs — s'no doubt she's wizard. Also one from Ron Dent (at Westcott). If you wish to know how far it is from one place to another in this dear England, don't expect an answer in yards or miles. Distance in this country is measured in distinct units:

(a) Minutes in the bus.

(b) Minutes by foot.

(c) Hours in the train — (if you can stand it.)

And another thing — when arranging to meet some 'sort' do not state a precise time, such as 'three fifteen'. Experience has shown me that the most advisable practice is to describe the limits of a period, say 'between two and three'. The reasons are numerous, but here's some:

(a) The first half dozen conveyances will probably be too crowded to be of service.

(b) There might be an air raid.

(c) It is quite likely that rain will fall as soon as you set out, which means rushing back for your coat.

(d) You are faced with the possibility of being challenged by a Service Police Corporal who will not be satisfied with a leave-pass, but will demand statutory declarations plus birth certificate! Also Berkshire is to be pronounced 'Barkshire' and Reading, 'Redding' — be on the alert for trickery! Also never ask for 'Scotch and soda' — you'll get 'Scotch and cider'. Just some tips for the newcomer.

> BOMBER BOYS:
> Evening shadows lengthen,
> Cheery voices
> Of the crews — heroes all
> Echo, through the trees
> NFTs are done, and tea — happy time!
> On dilapidated bicycles —
> Proud possessions, they go
> To briefing.
> Silent, listening, they sit while
> They are 'genned', —
> Darkness falls.
> Horrid Night!
> Engines suddenly
> Shatter its silence.
> Coloured lights — awful fairyland,
> Mark the airfield.
> Giant aircraft, blue exhausts,
> Roll, like huge black monsters,
> To the 'Taxi Post',
> Split-second timing,
> One by one, off they go,
> Lost in blackness.
> Silence.

Coffee, sandwiches, fleece-lined boots,
Men, machinery, guns and charts,
High above villages, streams and towns —
Icy, moonlit sky —
Black demons,
All together.
Lie in the dark and listen.
Lie in your soft civilian beds.
Lie —
Their's is one debt
You'll for ever owe.
Lie in the dark and let them go —
Lie in the dark and listen.

D. W. Scholes

Thursday 30 March: Base – Goole – Peterborough – Wallingford Bridge – Northampton – Bombing Ranges – Base.

A very good trip at 10,000 above cloud most of the way. I/C went U/S, but it was fixed OK.

We also do another flip at night at 12,000. Base – Northampton – Newquay – Aberdovey – Worcester – Northampton – Bombing Ranges – Base. We land at about 0120.

Tonight the boys go to Nuremburg and are diverted to the South of England on return. They arrive there to find a clamp so scatter to get in wherever they can, if they can for their fuel is by this time very low. At about 0500 a Halibag gets in here OK. At 0520 another Halibag tries but prangs. By mere inches he misses the main hangar, clips the trees, goes straight through main stores and spreads all over the field beyond. I have never seen such a mess. The rear gunner was the only one to come out alive. The crate broke in two just forward of the mid upper. The forward end of the fuselage was absolutely shattered to match-wood. One wheel whipped across the ground some 70 yds, to crash right through a garage. Strangely enough there was not much fire. In any case there was nothing big enough whole to burn very well. It's a rotten shame to see this happen. Here's a bloke gone all the way to the target and back through very hell and because of someone's stupidity they all, bar one, are lost — and a good A/C. These aren't the only ones tonight, a great number prang I am told. In addition 96 are lost in combat — the greatest losses of Bomber Command for the war.

31 March/1 April: We do a 'Bullseye' at 16,000. Base – Southwold – London (Green Park – target) – Bodmin – Penbroke – Stoke-on-Trent – Leicester – Bombing Range – Base.

A good trip all round although we have a bit of trouble with oxygen. We see no fighters. Searchlights do not get us much. We get a 38 yd error with the first stick of bombs and 90 with the second which are both a good show. Icing in cloud at first is bad, but we are above it all the way round after the climb. Over Wales it runs out to begin again further North. We bomb from 10,200 feet. Our error is converted to 20,000.

Saturday 1 April: We eventually arise after dying for some 9 hours. After lunch we set out on our bikes for Blisworth and catch a train to London. We make the nine miles in just under 40 mins and arrive half dead. We catch the old train and stand, repeat stand to London, where we immediately taxi to the Strand Palace Hotel. Our rooms are simply wizard — should be more of this! After a clean up we go to the Boomerang Club for tea, which as usual is bang on! Afterwards we visit Codger's Club, where the session begins — the beginning of the end. Supper we find pretty pucka at Mick's Cafe. Anyway finally we get home and tumble into bed, and die once again.

Sunday 2 April: Lunch at Boomerang Club and we get down towards Haymarket to the Plaza theatre and see 'Standing Room Only' — damned funny show. To get in we stand in a huge queue about 100 yds long. Periodically during our wait, old fellows, absolute down-and-outers come along to put on their acts before taking their hat down the queue. Some have fiddles, some organs, one or two just simply grind away — singing I guess. The best exhibition is put up by a fellow who bashes hell out of three tin cans strung to his belt. What a country!

The Boomerang Club sees us again for tea. We taxi to Euston and catch the 7.05 to Northampton. Here we taxi to Blisworth, after much panic to get hold of it. In Northampton there are oodles of Yanks and, poor show, oodles of young females out with them. Who are the most dangerous, those out in the more 'suburban' area amongst the trees and 'avenues'? At Blisworth we get our bikes and in the local we have some sandwiches and a drink before setting off home. It takes us about 1¼ hours, and we just arrive before the rain!

Wednesday 5 April: Last night at about 0200, 36 Dakotas came in. This morning we all got quite a shock to find 'em all over the airfield. It seems to us all that things are coming to a head quite quickly now, and the big event won't be long in coming off. All screened people are crewed up now.

Often we have 'full scale' exercises, 'in case'. There is a possibility that we shall do a few ops in Wimps — heaven forbid!

Thursday 6 April: Last night 25 Lancasters from 463 and 467 Squadrons (RAAF) were diverted here through very poor visibility, rain and drizzle. They all got in OK. It was a shaky do for the boys when they returned here. It was raining and the cloud base was about 500 ft — poor show indeed. Somehow they all landed! After tea we set off for a 'quiet evening' (briefing was scrubbed). Bill, Des, Darkie, Mike Madigan (Watson's Nav) and myself go to Syresham and on to Helmdon, the rest go to Towcester. Both parties have a satisfactory night. (Jock especially!) On return my radiator runs amuck and fuses all the lights — great panic. Eventually we fix things and have toast, butter and honey before going to bed.

Sunday 16 April: For the past 10 days things have gone much the same with bags of flying and now the time has come when we have finished except for the trimmings. The prospect of 14 days leave is wonderful. I shall go to Scotland. We had a bad time one night last week when at 20,000 ft we got mixed up in a thunder storm. Eventually we landed at Catfoss (CCS). Later the same night we returned here to base. We had a good night at Westbury on Friday last. I got a puncture on the way home and arrived back at 0530 hours!

Friday 21 April: We have finished here now thank goodness and are ready for a little leave any time. I have a good crew and with reasonable luck I can see no reason why we should fail to complete all our future operations on Lancasters successfully.

Saturday 22 April: I have been recommended for a commission. We leave here at about 1200 and at Brackley have lunch after checking our baggage through to Scampton, where we are to report on May 3rd.

Rolling pennies down the street causes untold panic in any English town. The kids go stone mad and chase them everywhere. Even adults in bus and shop queues have half a mind to chase them. They are certainly excited! We have a few ales before the train goes and the trip down is very bright. At London I have time for tea at the Boomerang Club and a few drinks at Codger's Club before my train to St Boswells at 9.25 pm. I get a seat OK with some very rowdy ATC twirps. At Carlisle I change trains to the Edinburgh (0630 hours) train. I chat to a WAAF to St Boswells. When I say chat it was a chat plus. She sat on my right side and spreads a rug across our knees. After a while I feel her hand on my right leg above the knee and so on. So I do the same with her left leg. This goes on until I get out at St

Boswells — don't know her name but we get to know each other pretty well.

Sunday 23 April: A very posh lady with a wee dog offers to take me as far as 'Monteviot' in her taxi. This is very much appreciated for apart from being just what I need I pay exactly nothing and, I'm in Scotland now! They meet me at 'Woodside' with the usual great ado. Everything I find just the same and inside a few minutes I feel that I have been here for days. I have a sleep first and then after tea I take a stroll up into the woods with 'Peter'. Spring is certainly here and everything is green and in bloom. The wild rhododendrons are particularly colourful. The elms are just in bud and the woodpidgeons are feeding on the young buds and make good shooting. I am quite tired and I have an early night after walking to the bus with Kath and Euph.

Monday 24 April: Up early and I feel much better. We go across to Jedburgh in the car. Here I am able to buy a few dry flies. (I choose Hardy's, Greenwell's, March Brown and Olive Quill.) We have a few sips at the Spread Eagle Hotel before going out to see a few farmers on the Estate. On the way home I shoot a crow off the nest and also another crow further on. It's quite late when we have had tea and after a game of dominoes and supper I have another early night. The weather has so far been lovely with bright sunshine each day and a slight cool west breeze. It seems as though it will continue to stay fine for a while yet too. This Scotland place is really the shot!

Tuesday 25 April: All morning I go shooting with Tom and also in the early afternoon. Soon after tea I go down to the river to give the fish a go. The gear isn't the best but it serves the purpose. I succeed in rising 6 fish during the evening and land none, but somehow they have me tricked on the strike. There is a rather annoying breeze blowing all evening making casting most difficult. The line is a little dry too and does not float well. There are many fish rising in the sheltered still water but they are very cunning and very shy. On the opposite bank near the junction of Ale and Teviot somebody is hard at it! Although I return home empty-handed, I am extremely happy. Fly fishing is such a pastime that one forgets absolutely everything except the trout — to forget at a time like this is sometimes most difficult. In any case catching anything is a secondary consideration.

Wednesday 26 April: I take Peter 'up the wood' after the usual egg and bacon breakfast and shoot the covers near the old dam. I bung cartridges in all directions until the gun barrels are quite warm. Things certainly get a pasting. These damned squirrels are hard to shoot. After lunch I set off down to the river again. I do no good in the slow water although I rise some fish. However further up in the faster water I catch 6 fish the longest about 14½ in which, for this stream is a very nice fish! I take them all on March Brown and Greenwell's Glory. At about 1730 I return for tea.

After tea I go down again with Euph. This time I fish the top col — but no show. There is a slight breeze again, making casting difficult. I leave Euph and fish the bottom col still to no avail. Quite suddenly the fish go down and it's all over. As I return up the hill I catch odd glimpses of owls and bats in the gathering darkness. Sometimes a frightened rabbit scampers away. Why I wonder do I think now of Pat? It is almost dark and the moon is rising when I get back. I have a goose egg for supper!

Friday 28 April: I shoot over open burrows again in the morning. It's very hot today — lovely. After lunch I take Peter up the back wood and shoot three rabbits in two shots (running!) I also belt down two wood pigeons and a pair of owls. I find a hen woodcock nestling its fluffy pair of youngsters amongst some brown leaves. Their colour blends magnificently with the leaves. Back at the house I take some photos of the dogs, and all of us together. I pack, have a bath, and prepare for the coming trip in the dust van.

About 7 pm they drive me to the Denham bus stop. I say goodbye most sadly. Really I should like to stay here indefinitely. Scotland shall always be my second home. The Macs give me a wizard departing meal of eggs and chops. They drive me to Hawick and we meet the 11.25 pm train eventually at about 1.10 am for it has had a breakdown near St Boswells. They won't leave me although I ask them not to wait on. At length I get in and I'm away towards London.

Saturday 29 April: I do not sleep much on the way down. The compartment is too stuffy. I see some Forts taking off on a raid somewhere near Wittering. At about 10.30 we pull in at Euston Station. My stay in Scotland has been even more successful than the first time. The Macleans are really lovely people in all ways. I shall always remember them as such. More than this they can give me what I live for — some 'life in the mountains' away from all the rest of the world for a little while.

Sunday 30 April: I meet Snake and Serps at Boomerang — as usual I am late.

Monday 1 May: At 1100 we set out to shop. First we go to Hardy's but find it isn't any more because of a recent bomb. At their new address we order a 'Perfect' reel each. The rest of the morning we spend buying all types of fly tackle running into some pounds worth, and I order a new rod.

Lunch at the Boomerang Club. A similar afternoon is spent. I am very happy being with Snake again. I buy Pat a seven pound, seven shilling brooch at Army and Navy stores. Lady someone picks us up somewhere near the Pickle Factory — what a do! Tea at Boomerang and we go to 'For whom the Bells Toll'. — Good show.

Wednesday 3 May: A squirt is putting on a regular act overhead and thoroughly amazes Snake. The speed is uncanny and must be seen to be believed fully. This one is the DH100. More I cannot put in this book. If Jerry's jet-crates look and fly as well as this then he's got something big also. I lunch with Snake at the Boomerang Club. The rest of the boys I fear have gone from there.

Thursday 4 May: At 1600 I catch my train to Lincoln from Kings Cross. At 1820 I change at Grantham and at 2110 I arrive at Lincoln. After a little supper I bus to Scampton where I get in with little trouble. The crew are full of beans and stories of their leave and I am glad to see them all again. Lancs from 619–617 are operating tonight and are on take off now, at about minute intervals.

Friday 5 May: This place is really bang on. The food is really wizard for RAF. It was this Squadron, 617, that did the big dam-busting show. Waddington 467 & 463 RAAF, where I hope to go, is quite nearby. They are giving us a big gen session here mostly on Lancasters. A/C from the group airfields Ingam, Dunholme Lodge, Waddington, Skellingthorpe, East Kirby, Ossington, Fiskaton, Bardney and so on are always overhead doing NFTs. At dusk we see them going out in great numbers. I believe that the invasion will not be long now. This is a permanent station built many years ago. It is only a few miles East of Lincoln, the cathedral can be seen on clear days straight down the road outside. At the moment they are rebuilding the runways and are nearly finished and 617 will shift back here soon from Ingam. The only A/C on the place are one Tiger Moth and a Puss Moth! Late this afternoon Geoff and I and Bill Watson Alf and Bruce wizz into Lincoln to catch the 1700 train to Nottingham where in heavy rain we get a taxi and get accommodation at the Milton's Head Hotel.

We race out around the pubs after tea and have a few. Nottingham I find quite an interesting place as far a an overseas serviceman is concerned. There is plenty of entertainment here and plenty to see of interest. I shall return here again.

Saturday 6 May: We spend the morning looking around the shops and then catch my train back to Lincoln and bludge in on someone's taxi to Scampton.

Friday 12 May: Decide to use the few days leave in Hampshire to check out some fishing. Get the morning London train and taxi straight to Hardy's in Pall Mall to get a lend of a rod and basic tackle from Harold. I set off by train to Andover where I book at The Crown — a small and not so flash a pub that I might look odd with my rod bag. After checking my map and the bus times, I make plans for the next two days, have a nice evening meal, sit at the bar and then bed.

Saturday 13 May: The Whitchurch bus takes me to Hurstbourne Priors where four roads meet with a pub on one corner — that's all — and the road east to Whitchurch follows the Bourne on its left before crossing it about a mile and a half upstream. I walk up beside the houses described by Plunket Greene in 'Where the Bright Waters Meet' and go down a path to the little church amongst the oaks and beyond to the stream.

Because of the nettles I go downstream first, put the rod together, tie on the Iron Blue Dun that Harold recommended and fish my way up the little brook which never exceeds ten yards across with patches of long streamer-weed varying from one to three feet in length. I catch nothing, so back to the pub for ale and cheese. After this I go down the road to the little bridge over the Bourne, climb over the fence and fish along the clear left bank. Here I catch my first English trout and miss another on the strike. The twelve inch trout I put back. A good day.

Sunday 14 May: Today I take the bus to the little town of Stockbridge and walk along the road towards Houghton. After about a mile the Test comes close to the road so I get over the stone wall, where there are no trees, to take a look. This is just a big Bourne to me, much more like the size of a river I'm used to. The other side seems much more open in parts, but I have all day with biscuits in my pocket so just keep on going skirting the rough bits, sitting, looking and fishing little open runs clear of weeds. I only see half a dozen trout rising, two of which I catch on a Red Tag, both much bigger than Yarra fish, which gives me much pleasure. Just before I get opposite the little church across the roadway at the end of Houghton village the river comes very close to the road, so I pack up, look down at the longish little town and get a ride back to Stockbridge with a farmer in his old cart. He is only too pleased to help, tells me where he lives, and to come any time. John Clark's his name.

Standing on the stone bridge at Stockbridge, looking downstream on the left side a trout rises within easy reach, if I was on the bank, but on the upstream side, although the bank is high and reedy just below the house, there is another one. The place seems deserted so over the wall I go and quickly try my Red Tag. He takes it and there I am only thirty yards from the bridge on somebody's place with a trout of a bit over a pound. Am I pleased to find John Clark up on the bridge laughing. He puts the fish in his canvas shoulder-bag with a bit of newspaper. He's never seen fly fishing before and I've made a friend. 'Blackwood Mill' is the name of his place and I'm going there tomorrow. So ends my poaching on the Test. Haven't seen any of those yellow-winged flies I've heard about. All those I've seen here are like small fluttering moths that get stuck on the surface every so often.

Pack up again and catch the number eighty six bus back to Andover.

Monday 15 May: John's farm is near Chilbolton and I decide to take the bus to Amesbury and back in the morning. A nice little place on the Avon river which is bigger than the Test. Wish I was stationed around here.

After a ploughman's lunch I set off for Clark's which is actually quite close to the Test river before you get to Chilbolton — upstream, and there's channels divide, one going round and the other through the town. Meet Mrs Clark and her sister and two land girls, Molly and Sue. I get on famously with Sue straight away. She seems to think Australia is a great place. John has sheep and breeds pigs. After tea we play dominoes and drink cider. John and his brother once tossed a coin to see if they would come to Australia. It came down saying no, but John who's called Jack by some, says he's been digging ever since. Eventually he takes me back to Andover in his little Bedford truck. The country around Chilbolton is nice and so is the river.

Tuesday 16 May: Get the eleven fifteen train to Paddington. Go straight to Hardy's and tell my tale. Good blokes. Then to the Boomer. Then to Kings Cross and get the 1605 to Lincoln. Then Scampton, where I find we are posted to 1654 HCU Wigsley on Stirlings.

Thursday 18 May: We all go hunting for a suitable engagement present for Darkie and Joan. We get a solid silver ash tray and cream bowl (engraving To Ron and Joan with best wishes from the 'Aussies') all for about ten pounds. They are really lovely things. Lunch we have at the Milton's Head. Jock has his eye on some piece in a red coat. I drink dry ginger only. Jock and I go and see 'Phantom of the Opera' with Nelson Eddy at the Odeon — damned good show, bang on all round. We have our tea at the 'Black Boy Grill'. The meal is really lovely and we both thoroughly enjoy it. I wish Pat was here too. We then catch our train at 2000 to Lincoln then 2130 bus to Scampton.

Saturday 20 May: We leave Scampton per bus for 1654 HCU Wigsley in the early afternoon. The drive is very pleasant and we arrive at about 1600. The place is not at all attractive and we all take an immediate dislike to it. The mess is particularly objectionable and the food is not good. We sleep in Laing huts about ½ mile from anywhere else. There is no water and washing facilities are a long way away. Rod, Bill Watson and I get in the same hut. There are also four Englishmen in with us from F/O Walkup's crew. The camp on the whole then is very much dispersed and I am truly thankful that I still have my bike.

Sunday 21 May: Parade at 0900 and we get a lecture by the CO, CI and CGI. The CI, W/C McFarlane is a firey Scot (3 tour man) and is very outspoken and severe in manner. Although he knows all about everything he is not a man that one can like immediately as such. After this we begin our series of gen lectures which is the most important thing for us for the first few days.

All about the airfield there are Stirlings in various states of prangery — some are complete write — offs, others still repairable. They have had a great number of prangs lately, mostly fatal and this is not encouraging at all. These aircraft are not built for this job at all. All they can expect is prangs. However, not so this chicken! I have a lot to live for, perhaps too much. I love every minute of this living business and I'm afraid I'm not at home at war. Most prangs are due to carelessness, of this I am certain. I say most, so therefore if I go it shan't be if I am any judge, through carelessness.

Wednesday 24 May: Today I get my Engineer, Jack Foreman from Kings Lynn in Norfolk. He has done some 20 hours so far in Stirlings and has done well. I like him on sight which is a good thing. As time goes on I shall get to know him as I have the whole crew. He will be a key man and must be a thorough gen man. Things going according to plan. These damned Stirlings are not a nice aeroplane and I have no confidence in them. However I shall not let myself be tricked by something duff — oh no!

Saturday 27 May: Today is a lovely day indeed with clear bright blue skies and a hot sun. The trees are in green now and the grass high. The smell of flowers is strong in the air and there is the constant sound of bees. After tea we battle off into Saxilby, a small attractive little village. All but Darkie come along and we have a fine time at The Anglers. Afterwards we go to the dance and have a good time there also. Riding home afterwards in the half light of midnight is particularly enjoyable and the smell of hawthorn blossom is terrific. Bill and Jock cart a pair off home tonight —one each that is. On their way home they see a Lancaster crash in flames and explode. They return at about 0130 hours.

Sunday 28 May: Another very lovely day — too fine a day for war, far too fine — still, we fly.

Tuesday 30 May: It seems my commission will all be fixed up here. I have got to know Jack much better and consider myself very fortunate in getting him. He is a gen man, keen, quick and alert. He is 19 years old. I like him a lot. His 'better half' lives in Goole (Yorkshire). Tonight we whip down to Normanton for a beer but the bloke won't come to row us across the Trent so we have had it. I ring the Bridge at Saxilby and order a meal for us all so we turn round and ride all the way back there. The meal is worth it however — beautiful! (Reminds me of the Olde Bull but not as good nearly.)

Thursday 1 June: Another month has passed away, a month I'll never forget. We get the afternoon off— the hours for the month have been satisfactory so the CO gives us the time off.

We have a quick lunch, bike to Swinderby, and catch the 1317 to Notts. Bill and I, in our high class way as usual get in at the Victoria. The rest stay at the YMCA. We eat at the Overseas Club. At the Black Boy we meet a Yank glider tug pilot and have some grog with him before adjourning to the Palais de Dance. He is an unusually decent type of Yank. We all get quite merry. We have a good time with all and sundry at the dance. Bill carts some bag off afterwards. There's no beer at the dance.

Sunday 4 June: Do a spot of flying — up to the Wash and back doing 2 and 3 engined flying a few overshoots and a landing — all OK. Quite a good meal tonight too — s'funny! Invasion soon now I bet. This station is 'prepared'.

Monday 5 June: Rome falls. All are full of hope and hearts are happy today. Bomb loads are at the crates.

Tuesday 6 June: D-DAY Everybody flies today! We do a decoy to Dieppe Coast. The day is not good, there is low cloud and some higher with a falling barometer. Still they go across. The Second Front is on. All England is ringing with the news I bet. All aircraft taking part in this show have broad black and white bands painted across each wing and around the fuselage. They are 18" across and can be clearly seen. God I hope we can finish it soon now. There is a lot I could write about concerning this invasion business but I cannot be bothered. I knew it was coming fast. All England was prepared some little time ago now. They have worked hard day and night. Every man woman and child has had a job and now they have all another job in addition to their old one. They are doing fine. After what I have seen at dawn — the first grey streaks of dawn, today good luck to the Army down below and the Navy too, that stands off Cherbourg. That golden, inevitable human bridge across the choppy channel waters, green and ugly.

'They shall not grow old as we, who are left grow old' —

Friday 9 June: Circuits and twitches. Duff weather. Into Saxilfurkin for tea at the Bridge — grilled chops! Bang on show as usual. Early morning detail tomorrow! so bed.

Saturday 10 June: Decoy to Fecamp Coast.

Sunday 11 June: Air test in the morning. After lunch, we go up and do some practice corkscrews with a Martinette. After tea Bill and I bike to Harley where I send a wire to Pat and one home. I also buy countless stamps. The local pub is a frightful dump. The little place is particularly vile and boy! she's antique. Back for supper at YM and go to bed.

Monday 12 June: Wet dinghy drill at Larnham in the early morning. I book in at the Bridge Inn, Dunham for tea on the way home. About 1930 hours the bomber stream sets off for Dunham — double bacon and eggs plus a couple of hard boiled in our pockets. There's a prang on the way home (Manning) Geoff prangs one egg in his pocket when he gets home belting Jock up!

Tuesday 13 June: Duff morning. Airborne at about 1800 hours but pancake immediately because of bad fuel leak from st'd inboard distributor into fuselage. Get in OK — not a very pleasant show at all. All that is needed is a single spark — ! I am getting worried about Pat. A year has passed now since we have been together. We have done well. I shall never change. Every day I am more certain of this. Every girl I see or meet, which is now a daily occurrence, I compare with her. They are all duff. The English girl is a queer creature — so fickle minded, and so simple. There are odd exceptions, but still these seem a little artificial I think. Time might beat me, this is my great fear. If I live to see Aussie again it will be in no small way due to Pat's influence on me. I have a lot to live for, I believe, and I am very careful. My crew too have so much to live for. They are such decent chaps, all of them. Their lives are in my hands. No doubt if I get mail from Pat again soon I shall forget this stuff and kick myself for being so dull, but, until then I shall wonder on. Without Pat what is there in future old man? You thought you wouldn't go this way eh? Come in suckers they say. She's the loveliest and sweetest girl I have ever met and I have met a few in my wanderings through Aussie, New Zealand, America and these British Isles. Still, if I read back through her mail how can I even think of these things? Still again, why this break in mail? Cable her, mug, cable her!

The beachhead in Normandy is going OK. Duff weather is a nasty set back though. Bomber Command are doing a lot of French trips now and the boys are all for it! There are some daylights on too now, mostly 6 Group Halibags. The Yanks have done and are still doing a magnificent job on land and in the air. The 47, 38 and 17 have proved themselves good aircraft in combat.

I have grown used to England now and am even tired of it. I wanna go back where I belong!

Friday 16 June: Corkscrews with Rod Mellowhip (since killed over Russelheim). On N/F and do circuits and twitches at Waddo (467 & 463) with McCubbin. Obstruction on runway at base and later at Waddo. (Jig goes through the fence! — damn him.) Geoff goes on 16 with Middleton, damn him too!

Wednesday 21 June: Out of bed late, bags of panic with 3 days T Parade! Stirling prangs inside circuit due to fire in starboard mainplane. Hell of a bloody mess. Three killed and four injured seriously. This should never never have happened. I have a parachute and am not afraid to use it if the need ever arises. Take some photos in the afternoon out at G-George. They should be good.

On N/F. Go to Eppestone to bomb, but not permitted to bomb from Code A minus 2000. However A/C on Ex 13 and climb through cloud from 4 five to 10 four. Base – Squire's Gate – St Bee's Hd. – Drem – Prior's Hardwick – Base. 5.35. Home on lattice lines and break cloud at 1000' — 1200', join circuit and pancake. Pretty good trip all round.

Friday 23 June: I go by tender across to Swinderby (51 Base) for an interview with the AOC, Air Commodore Bussel. I find him a very nice fellow and am satisfied. My commission should not take so long now. I put in a word about 467 Squadron and this seems to be OK. Tonight we do a trip with McCubbin. We get coned over Hull and engaged by a Spitfire. It is a very good trip all round and things go fine. Mac and I both land the old tub. Whole trip done at 13000'. We bomb TI (Red) at Newcastle —dead on heading 075°.

Saturday 24 June: Miss out on Ex 16 — A/C U/S. After eggs and bacon we go to bed about 2400 hours. This place is a thorough bind — a thorough stink of an airfield if ever there was one. A stick of cookies should go across it. The Stirling is a rotten aeroplane. Amen!

Tuesday 27 June: T/O late on Ex 16 — S/C to intercept concentration at the third turning point at 15000'. 'George' goes U/S at about 8 five in the climb. I order the crew to fix parachutes. Another A/C misses us by mere inches during the following attempts to fix things up. Geoff accidentally jettisons the rear escape hatch — I wonder where it landed! This is the nearest thing that I have been yet to bailing out. The rest of the trip is quite ropey. We bomb at Eppestone on return to base. Pancake in daylight.

Wednesday 28 June: We are told that we must do the trip again which shakes all of us rigid. McCubbin gives us a little natter about it all and I agree that it will be the best thing to do. It does make us all mad though for otherwise we should have gone on leave today. However perhaps everything does happen for the best, Des's chart and log are by no means masterpieces. The thing that hurts me most perhaps is the fact that I shall now miss out on the posting to Syerston with Rod and all the rest of the chaps. Will pick them up at the Squadron no doubt. I'm really cheesed, that's the point. I wanna go back to Pat.

Saturday 1 July: Spanner goes into hospital with the flu. 'The boys' come back from leave.

Tuesday 4 July: W/C Rollo Kingsford-Smith DSO, DFC and Spam comes to be CFI. We do 16 at last — half way to Holland. Run out of oxygen near Newcastle. Bill does a little flying. We are finished with Stirlings! Posted to Lancaster Finishing School, Syerston.

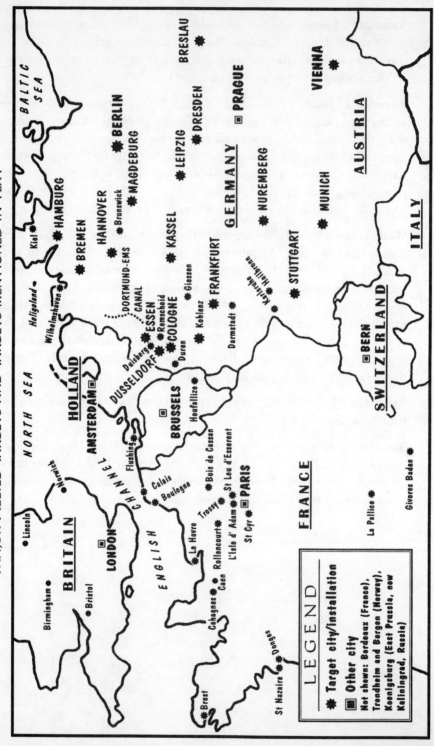

MAJOR ALLIED TARGETS AND TARGETS MENTIONED IN TEXT

PART 4

BOMBER COMMAND OPERATIONS

Friday 7 July 1944: Wolverhampton is a nice little township although built all higgledy-piggledy, up and down hill. The shops are quite clean also the streets and the people seem quite nice types. I like it far better than its large neighbour, Birmingham. The pubs are quite decent as we find out tonight and the beer quite good.

Saturday 8 July: During the morning rain falls and we spend our time looking through the shops. After lunch we catch the bus back to Birmingham, a very interesting drive, where we go looking for cherries and tomatoes in the market square and eventually succeed.

We have tea at Darkie's place — very good too, although I get up feeling as though I could eat more! Now this sort of Darkie's. To me she appears to be a very quiet innocent and plain girl. I should say she would be very old-fashioned in the things that are most modern today. However, although not striking to look at I am sure she is very good natured and decent. Obviously she doesn't know the score, but as Darkie hasn't that many more clues, they should make a fine Birmingham city couple. We catch our train to Nottingham via Derby where we find we are stranded due to our train being late and missing the connection. We sleep on the seats! A slashing little piece in green from the Services Canteen makes us some tomato sandwiches with those we bought at Birmingham.

Sunday 9 July: We finally set off for Syerston after the usual amount of messing about. The station we find bang on just as we had been told. Our quarters are champion and the food good.

Monday 10 July: Numerous boring talks fill the day. We go to 'Dive Bomber' in the evening at the station cinema.

A bloke comes home, p—d as a newt, having fallen in the Trent out of a boat!

Saturday 15 July: For the past few days we have all been doing extensive study and we are full of gen now and itching to get cracking.

Sunday 16 July: We do circuits and twitches at Woodhall Spa. The Lancaster is a fine A/C (but still I think there are 3 too many engines).

Tuesday 18 July: 3 Engined work and corkscrews at Waddington. It appears a wizard station and I hope to go there. I find the Lancaster a very easy aeroplane to fly and already have full confidence in it.

Thursday 20 July: Last night we did Ex 7 (ROA at 20,000') and landed at about 0100 this morning. Quite a good trip. Tonight we all cycle down to the Elm Tree and get very happy indeed. This is a darned nice little pub. One has to cross the Trent by punt in order to get to it. A dance floor is incorporated in the pub. Returning across the Trent is terrifying to say the least. The hill that has to be climbed to the main road is a dead loss too. However we have a super time and I say again this is a hell of a good pub.

Saturday 22 July: We get up and dash about getting clearances and pack our stuff. We are posted to 61 Squadron, Skellingthorpe. I am of course furious about it all, because I was almost certain that we would go to either 463 or 467 at Waddington. However all the bitching that I can do cannot change the situation, and off we go in the bus. We arrive at Skelly in the early afternoon. Soon we are organised in our billet and we are taken down to the flights. B Flight is the flight we are in. The Squadron Commander is W/C Doubleday DSO, DFC and Spam. He is an Australian, coming from somewhere near Wagga — farm people I believe. He is a wizard fellow and I like him very much straight away, when he has a little yarn with us all in his office. I am sure we shan't be too badly off here. It's not far to Lincoln, and 61 is better off than 50, the other squadron here, as convenience in position goes. We are quite near our messes and not far from the flights. This is not a peacetime station, but we are quite comfortable and there is no bull to put up with. The Squadron letters are QR (50 being VN). Well, 35 trips to do and I guess I'll know a good deal more about the game and, in general, everything!

Sunday 23 July: I get around the place looking out all the different things and places that will be of interest to me. I am down to do a 2nd Dicky tonight with the W/C. This is a good show, because I want to get it done and finished with. However, later on it is scrubbed so we go on a 6½ hour X-country instead finishing off with a little bombing. Des's oxygen goes for a burton at 20 thou so we go round at 12,000 which turns out OK.

Monday 24 July: Tonight Geoff and I are down to go to war. However after the Ops Meal Geoff's trip is scrubbed. I am to go with F/O Watkins, a very nice fellow who has 9 trips so far, which on the face of it doesn't sound so good because I'd rather go with the W/C or someone with a few more trips in.

The feeling at briefing is so queer. I expect I shall get used to it though. There are two targets tonight — Stuttgart and Donges. I am going to Donges to bomb oil storage tanks, not far from St Nasaire. Eventually we get out to the crate QRY Yoke and do a run up. The waiting before T/O is what I find most trying. At length we get in for the last time and start the engines again. We taxi away. All round the perimeter track A/C are taxying slowly down towards the caravan, where crates are turning onto the runway at about 1 per minute. We get down there after a long taxi. All the people from the station are here to see them off. I see my crew there amidst them all. The feeling is somewhat like that feeling when one leaves dear old Australia on a troopship. We turn into wind and take off, climb and circle the airfield before setting course for the first TP — down near Reading somewhere. Well this is it.

On course we climb slowly. Up through a thin sheet of st. cu. cloud and all is clear above except for the odd whisp of cirus. The sun has set and the sky is a weird blue-grey as we climb on. By the English coast we are almost at height and far below I see the Sussex coast slide slowly from sight behind me. That funny feeling comes into ones middle again and a lump comes in the throat. On we go out across the channel. Then quite suddenly all the nav lights that have been burning steadily around us, go out one by one. We are alone now — just a lot of bodies in a great whirling machine. Darkness comes suddenly. We cross the French coast near St Malo. All is quiet. On we go, nothing happens. Then, far ahead and to starboard I see some flak bursts and several searchlights flick on and weave about in the blackness. We begin to window and weave slightly as we approach the scene, but we are well to port. The place is Lorient so we are more or less on track. We are not fired at for we are well beyond range. Other aircraft however are in range and we are being continually engaged. We run on down SW and go out across into 'the Bay' to turn further port, running to the coastline. Past St Nasaire we turn inland S of the target to the last turning point before running in. The feeling of excitement becomes more intense as I look at the watch — 15 minutes before H hour. At H-11 the fun begins and we are near the turning point. Great strings of yellow cascading illuminating flares go down as PFF locate the target. Over the VHF the Controller and Deputies can be heard. A red TI goes down as a proximity marker. We turn towards the target. Other Lancs are all round us, their four silver exhausts showing up. The marking is not going well. The pilot begins to weave more violently as flak becomes more intense and the risk of fighters is now greater. Another RedTI goes down. We are almost there and still no marking down. There is nothing that can be done but orbit. This is an awful business — hundreds of A/C circling waiting to bomb, and no one can see anyone else. The collision risk is very great. Another A/C narrowly misses us and passes overhead.

The greens are down at last. The Controller calls them away with Tally Ho, and calls us in to bomb the greens. Here we go on the run up, the sight is terrific. Searchlights come from nowhere. We are at 9,000 ft. We weave violently towards the markings. Flak is coming up more now. I see a PFF A/C coned below and to port and they are giving him merry hell, however he escapes — good show! Now we are almost there. Never have I ever experienced such a feeling of tense excitement as this. The whole sky is lit up with weird lights — just like a ten times glorified Henley Night. Bombs burst with vivid white flashes. Flak is all around, and light flak, like snakes, comes up to meet us in long red streams. We steady up for the bombing run. It seems ages. One feels like a sitting pigeon, so exposed or like a man walking across Piccadilly with no trousers on would feel. At length the bombs go, and the crate shudders as they leave the carriers. Away we go again weaving violently with much power on. We narrowly miss being caught in the fork of two probing searchlights, as we run out of the target. On we go straight up to 11 to the coast inland. 'Well, we are OK so far', is the way I feel. Eventually we reach the French coast again after what seems hours and hours. Away over on the starboard side I can see gun flashes from the front line and I wonder how they're going down there really, after all the papers are full of the better side of the picture. I also see V-1 in action.

Out across the channel we go heading for England. There it is. How relieved I feel when I see those friendly searchlights of London and Bristol. We cross the coast near Portsmouth and come up country to the right of Bristol. Some forty minutes later we arrive over base and soon our turn to land comes, and we slip down to earth safe and sound — another Lancaster back home again, home again to go again. The crew-bus takes us back to the briefing rooms where we are interrogated. We give the intelligence types all the gen we can about the trip — the weather, the marking, defences on route and over the target, height, time, heading and speed when bombs went — indeed, everything. Off we go for our bacon and egg meal before bed. Everyone talks about the trip.

Well, if I have 34 more trips like this to do I must set about learning and learning more about my job. I must keep the crew up to scratch and keep out any tendency of over confidence. Every trip must be the first trip. With constant work, keenness, alertness and a little luck I think we shall be alright.

Tuesday 25 July: Off to war. Target St Cyr, where wireless parts are stored also much military equipment. Load 1 x 4000 HE 'Cookie' and 6 x 500 HE. We attack in daylight. A small piece of flak hits the B/As compartment. We see one crate go in, but 5 chutes open. Spitfires escort us and I only see 2 ME109s which do not attack.

I have now got my own A/C. QRW 'Willie' a Lanc III. She doesn't seem a bad old crate. Once we cross the enemy coast on the way home the trip becomes most enjoyable indeed for it is a lovely day and England looks so pretty in the sunshine — so does France for that matter, but the ugly black puffs specking the sky are very disconcerting and I am afraid I saw little of the French countryside in detail. W/C Doubleday leads us.

Wednesday 26 July: War. Target Givores Baden, a marshalling yard 12 miles south of Lyons in France. 9 x 1000 HE. Attack at night. It's an awful long way on paper. Off we go. Soon after crossing the French coast I see an A/C shot down. Poor chaps. We have to fly in atrocious weather to reach the target with lightning, hail, rain, and terrific bumpiness. We have to orbit in this weather. The boys put on their nav lights. I see two collide, and another hits a mountain. As we cannot see the TIs we turn for home planning to bring our load home again. Eventually after what seems an age of ups and downs cloud, lightning and odd flak we cross the enemy coast almost at dawn. We find it necessary to jettison our load to reach England, where we land, through fuel shortage, at an American airfield called Merryfield. After a meal and refuelling we fly back to base. This has been a dreadful trip and I never wish to do another like it. We sleep soundly until tea time. After tea we go down the road to the WVS hostel for supper. On the way home Geoff and I get some drops in our eyes at SSQ.

Friday 28 July: NFT in morning — low flying. War. Target Stuttgart. 'Cookie' and clusters. Attack at night. All the way from the enemy coast to the target I see A/C going down. Just a fine, glowing yellow light slowly falling earthwards with occasional spurts of orange flame. Down and down for what seems ages, then a terrific flash which lights the whole sky momentarily as it hits the earth — a horrible but fascinating sight. Just before we drop our bombs a 109 attacks, but a violent dive to port succeeds in shaking him off. Geoff doesn't fire either, but due to his alertness we live on. We turn for home, and, instead of returning home low, as briefed, I climb to 23 thousand and stay there. All the way home more crates go down. 2 are missing from here. 62 are lost from Gp out of 195.

Saturday 29 July: Up at 1400. Lecture by visiting padre. After tea we go into Lincoln per bike and see 'This Happy Breed'. On the way home we pause awhile on a seat beside a park to eat some fish and chips. There is an early morning 'do' on in the morning, so we go straight to bed. This operational life is fine in a way — so exciting, every minute of life seems so important. I think a lot of home and Pat. I must get through it all.

Sunday 30 July: War. Target Cahagnes (between St Lo and Caen). 700 A/C taking part. 13 x 1000 bomb load. Over target about 8/10 ths cloud and we are ordered down below the cloud base. However the mission is abandoned and the Hun gun positions, which are worrying our troops, go untouched. We have a good look at Cherbourg on the way home. We are ordered to proceed home via Pershore and Squire's Gate, in order to use sufficient fuel to lower the AUW to maximum landing!! Waste of petrol? By mistake I join Fiskaton circuit and land there with a full bomb load! However I take straight off again and return to base. Damned shame we couldn't bomb.

I have received my commission and so I battle off down to London to get all my stuff fixed up. I stay at the Strand Palace as usual. This step, although really important, seems to be an every-day occurrence to me. I am interested in but one thing — the completion of this tour of operations. And so I arrive back at the Squadron — a different uniform, a different mess, but not a different fellow. The new mess I find wizard, such a change to my old mess in which I have eaten for so long. I cable home and Pat.

Tuesday 1 August: War. Target Mont Candon, near Dieppe. 13 x 1000 (delay). Daylight. 10/10 cloud unable to bomb. Proceeded to 65m NE of Skegness to jettison before returning to base. It is a very lovely day with quite a warm sun shining, when we get back. Carry delays today!

Wednesday 2 August: War. Target Bois de Cassan. 13 x 1000, all delay. Daylight. Flak moderate, and two A/C blow up. We nearly collect a load of bombs. Bill cut his finger today and so we take another bloke — a Canuck, who is on his first trip. This is a bit unfortunate. However I expect Bill's finger will be OK soon. It is an awful gash he has nevertheless. Today is another lovely day, once the morning cloud disperses.

Des has been given his papers to fill in for his commission — good show. Des is a good navigator, of this I am now sure.

Thursday 3 August: War. Target Trossy. 15 x 1000 (4 x 6hr delay). Over target one crate was hit by flak and crashed, flaming down to earth, with another one. Nobody got out. The controller in a P38 packs us in close together. Spits provide the escort. Seemed a good prang. Bill's finger isn't too good and we take F/S Taylor, RAF as mid upper. He is a good type and a good gunner. It is very hot up in the air, and I find a pair of dark glasses protect my eyes from the glare.

We all go down to the Plough for a drink or two after tea and have a good old time together. We get some fish and chips, take them home, and devour them in a few moments!

Friday 4 August: Little local flying in the afternoon — HLB! We go into Lincoln for tea at the Saracen's Head (Snake-pit) after which we see 'Demobbed' — an English show, not too brilliant.

Saturday 5 August: Up at 0200 for meal and briefing. War. Target St Leu d'Esserent. 14 x 1000. Daylight. Again we have to take a spare gunner to fill Bill's place in the mid upper turret (Sgt Jebb). Fires his guns in dispersal! W/C Doubleday leads the squadron. This is a V-1 store again like the other targets lately have been. We get hit by flak in the starboard wing. This is the closest that the damned stuff has been to us yet, and I hope, the closest it will ever come to us. The attack goes well enough I suppose. Some small patches of cu. cloud make it difficult for the bomb aimers. We get ours away on the target area successfully however. Another lovely day. Big hole in wing.

Sunday 6 August: Up at 0700 for ops meal.

War. Target L'Isle d'Adam. 14 x 1000 V-1 store. Bad weather just before target splits the force and the fighter escort and just as we drop our bombs some dozen or 18 ME109s attack from the port quarter up out of the sun. The next few moments are unrememberable. I do remember seeing two Lancs go down and two Jerry pilots come floating past on the port side. I can see the black crosses on some of the 109s — too damned close. We formate with 7 other Lancs and at full power, climb to 20,000 into thin cirus which affords sufficient protection. Not until in sight of the English coast do we break up. Good show, home again. Coombes is missing. Damn this war business, I get cheesed writing about it. Afraid therefore that my notes about my ops are somewhat brief and inconcise, however all my life I shall remember every minute of every one of them.

We are due to go on leave tomorrow. I am looking forward to this break very much indeed. Of course I shall go to Scotland — to the country, the rod and the gun, farther away from war than anything in this world.

Monday 7 August: I go to London. I am on leave — 'how green is my valley'. I feel like an escaped prisoner or an animal let out into a new pasture. I stay at the Strand Palace. In the evening I have a few drinks and an early night. V-1 passes overhead throughout the night.

Tuesday 8 August: I fill in the day in one way or another and at 9.45 pm I catch my train for Scotland. The trip is quite uninteresting, boring and tiring, not to mention dirtying.

Wednesday 9 August: At about 1000 hrs I arrive at 'Woodside' and receive great welcomes from the Macs and the dogs. Of course Tom takes this opportunity of having a wee nip all round. I am very glad to see them. Inside a quarter of an hour after I arrived the boss has me out after a couple of woodpidgeons in the garden. It is a lovely Autumn day. The elms and oaks in the woods are losing their leaves. I change, have a meal, and off I go rambling with Tom and the dogs. I am very happy and find no trouble in forgetting all about aeroplanes — indeed everything, but what I am about.

Sunday 13 August: For the past few days I have been having the time of my life — seldom a moment without a gun in my hand or a dog at my side. The weather has been very considerate indeed with but an occasional shower. Tom and I went down to the top col one evening with the fly. He took a nice brown (wet) whilst I could only manage to take two small browns and lose a grayling!

One afternoon I went to Jedburgh in the car where I bought Pat some oddments — shoes, scarf and keepsakes. This morning I catch the bus to Edinburgh where I meet Bill, and later on Geoff and Jock. We stay at the Grand Hotel again. Most of our time we spend on the wee bottle, but I take this opportunity to go up to the castle and have a good look round. I find it most interesting and impressive especially the new war memorial. In the evening we go to a dance at the 'Locarno' — not too bad.

Monday 14 August: After buying some more oddments for Pat I pack the whole show up ready to post. We go off then to buy some socks, pyjamas, shirts etc. I buy Tom some socks and ties for his birthday. I catch a bus back to Ancrum. Tom is very pleased with my gift — we have a nip from the cupboard!

Wednesday 16 August: And so the time comes to go back to camp. Euph gives me some hard boiled eggs, tomatoes, cakes and sandwiches to take with me. It's damned hard to say goodbye to all this — in the back of my mind I cannot get the awful idea away that this could be my last leave!

Early this morning I catch the local puffing-billy to Edinburgh which only just gets me there in time for the 1000 hrs fast train to London. I find Bill and Geoff waiting for me and they have kept me a seat. Soon we are away. It turns out to be a lovely day, once the low cloud break up. We stop at Newcastle, York and at Grantham before we get out and catch our very slow, slow train back to Lincoln. We have tea at the Snake Pit. Here I learn that Rod Mellowship is missing since a raid on Russelheim. This shakes me to the core. Rod was such a wizard chap, and Ron Hare, the WOP was one of the best too. It seems that there were a lot of fighters about that night. This puts the finishing touches on my 'twitch' that has slowly been developing in me whenever I have thought of returning to camp. We cycle home and after a 'chat' with old 'Salamoe' we go to bed.

Thursday 17 August: War. Target Hanover — scrubbed, thank God!

Friday 18 August: War. Target Bois de Cassan. V-1 Bomb dump. 14 x 1000 no delay. Daylight. We manage to find and bomb the right target through scattered cu. cloud, thanks to Darkie. Returned base 1700 hours. Flak is moderate, but the wave behind us gets a fair amount tossed up at them. After tea we all go down to the WVS for supper.

Saturday 19 August: Up at 0200. War. Target La Pallice, oil storage tanks for U-boats and H/T. 12 x 1000. Daylight. A most tiring trip. The gaggle has to climb through broken stratus over the channel to reach B/H. At target there is unexpected layer cloud and we orbit port losing height to bomb. Darkie again saves the day and we bomb on the first run up. Flak over the target is quite accurate and, after we bomb, becomes intense. We get through untouched. We are diverted to Little Snoring, in Norfolk. (Mosquito MK 2s.) We have a meal and a couple of hours sleep before returning to base in shocking weather. We go to bed completely fagged out, for we have had about 4 hours sleep in the last 48. Showery weather continues with occasional thunderstorms throughout the night.

Monday 21 August: Roll bombs around am, lecture pm. Stood down until 0000 hrs. We go to Lincoln, and do a little shopping. Tea at the Savoy and then we see 'The Dessert Song'.

Tuesday 22 August: War. Koenigsburg — scrubbed. Rains like hell.

Thursday 24 August: War. Target Koenigsburg — scrubbed.

Friday 25 August: War. Target Darmstadt — City. 'Cookie' and clusters. 240 A/C. Night. Fire raid 240 x 4000 HE and 240,000 incendiaries. The controller makes an early return and the No. 1 & 2 deputies are shot down, so we orbit for 35 minutes while PFF try to mark. During this business I see a couple of rockets flying at terrific speed in the horizontal plane — most alarming things! Spanner is most alarmed. There are fighters about.

We get through it all OK. Fortunately there is a break in the searchlight belt between Mainz and Mannheim, through which we belt with 270 on the clock. F/O Church is missing on his 28th trip.

Saturday 26 August: War. Target Koenigsburg. 'Cookie' and clusters. Night. City, fire raid. (East Prussia.) This almost breaks my heart when we take off — we are diverted before we take off. There is the odd spot of flak over Denmark. Over Sweden, all lit up in a terrific blaze of lights and Neon signs, there is a magnificent display of 'friendly' flak, both heavy and light. Being briefed for 2 searchlights we arrive to find some 190 of the bleeding things. We weave in, bomb and get out somehow, I don't know, that's quite certain. The return is the same. At the Denmark coast we a/c for Lossiemouth in NE Scotland, however, after hours of flying at 2000 we cross the coast in daylight near Peterhead where I land at once, tired out completely body, mind and soul, after 11 hrs 25 mins flying and a mileage of approximately 2000.

I write a note to Pat.

Tuesday 29 August: War. Target Koenigsburg — again, oh hell!! (This may be as far as this diary will go.) 'Cookie' and clusters. Off we go and, although the route is slightly different, the trip in not much different until we reach the south east coast of Sweden, where we run into severe electrical storms which continue out over the Baltic Sea. Eventually we arrive in the vicinity of the target. The controller brings us down below C/B and I find too late, that we are port of track and so after orbiting and evading S/Ls, proceed as planned.

It was found necessary to execute this second attack as the first failed to burn out the centre of the city and the dock area. The object is political as well as direct support of the Russian troops. We cross the Danish coast in dawn light and it is early morning with an accompanying mist when we reach base — too late for a diversion. I land early and after taxying to dispersal at the end of the runway in use. Just as I am closing down I get the shock of my life — a 50 squadron crate passes over us at some 20 ft and crashes headlong into the wood not 50 yds from where we stand. This is surely fate, for we have all missed certain death by a hair's breath. How it misses us I really cannot ever tell. I shout to Darkie and Spanner to see if they can get anyone out of the steaming wreck — luckily it does not catch fire. I close down, but damned shakily and quickly! Everyone is OK except the nav is dead. Evidently the cause was the misty conditions, coupled with the loss of one outboard and inexperience.

Well we're home again, thank God!!

Thursday 31 August: War. Target Rollencourt. 14 x 1000 at 12000' V-1 Bomb dump. Daylight.

It is a shambles getting into our gaggle and we do not eventually reach our station until we cross the French coast. We make a dummy run, but successfully bomb on the second run up. Flak is light on our A/P but on the other one south east of us it appears much more intense. We dive away across the coast very fast and arrive back at base at about 2000 hrs. (The bombing was very good with a good concentration.)

After a chat in the hut we all turn in.

Tuesday 5 September: War. Target Brest. 12 x 1000 Gun positions hindering naval and military operations. Daylight.

We take off very late and don't see a crate until near the target where I see a couple going home. We therefore go across the target solo and have a good run up. Flak is negligible, but we are a piece of pie for any fighter. Everyone has landed when we get home!

Wednesday 6 September: After tea we set out with the intention of getting to the Ensa show, but instead, we wind up at The Plough in Skelly village. On the way home we buy some nice eating apples. I write home and to Pat.

Sunday 10 September: War. Target Le Havre. 14 x 1000 German troop positions and strongposts. Daylight. A damned fine show. Never have I seen such vivid proof of the awful destruction caused by a concentrated HE attack. Columns of smoke billow up to a great height while the bomb flashes are quite distinct through it, the ground waves too are easily seen. Somehow I feel sorry for the poor blokes down there below as we turn away. Nothing could live through such a bombardment or, if one did survive one would be insane for life I am sure. Never shall I forget this. Flak slight, but accurate.

Monday 11 September: War. Target Darmstadt. 'Cookie' and clusters. Operate at night. The first attack was not good enough.

I have never seen more fighter activity than tonight. All about us in the target area there is green tracer, snaking about probing into the darkness. Here and there a crate explodes and plunges down. On the run up Bill sees a 'Mossie' after a JU88. Just after leaving the target we narrowly miss colliding with another Lanc on the starboard beam. Spanner is speechless but luckily points, and I miss him somehow. The fighters are active all the way home and if I ever weaved and kept my eyes peeled, I do tonight. Flak is troublesome en route in and out. The moon rises, big and yellow as we cross the beautiful

English coast on the way home. At base I am surprised to find that no A/C are missing from 61. (50 lose some). (286,000 incendiaries + 210 'cookies' are dropped).

Tuesday 12 September: Tonight there is a war on but F/O Collins, an Aussie, takes my crate. I spend some time giving him all the gen I can. This is his first night op. Target Stuttgart. ('Cookie' and clusters). We watch T/O from the 'wagon'. R–Roger loses 2 engines (inners) on T/O and prangs at the end of the runway (070°) — the bombs do not explode, for I'm writing this!

Wednesday 13 September: I awake early to see if 'Willie' is home. I find it came back on 3, having had the starboard outer shot out over the target by flak. It is on a star inspection and not cat. A/C to my great relief. Although an old tub, I have learnt to have a kind of affection and trust in her. We are stood down about midday so after tea we go to Lincoln and see the show 'Music While you Wait', put over — not bad.

I write letters on return until I am too tired to continue with them — or, even this!

Friday 15 September: War. Target Brunswick — scrubbed.

Sunday 17 September: War. Target Boulogne. 14 x 1000 Germans! Operate in daylight.

In the beautiful, sunny, clear morning we T/O and gaggle across over Ipswich to the target. Here I nearly have my time again. Flak, although not intense, is extremely accurate. The crates on my port bow are all hit on the run up. All I can do is sit and wait my turn. Sure enough up she comes on our port, bang on predicted stuff. How we are missed I don't know. Someone is hit ahead and an outer engine complete comes rushing past just below us, the crate plunges into the fields and explodes. However, the famous 5 Gp bombing of Le Havre is repeated. On return we do find a couple of small holes in the elevators and near Geoff's turret. F/O Boland, an Aussie, put up a magnificent show. Although wounded in the right leg and left arm, he returned on 3 and put down a wizard landing before collapsing. (The B/A, too, was wounded.) His chute-harness was cut away by shrapnel — one piece lodged in his cigarette case. Lucky lad!

After tea I write home and to Pat and finally, pack my bag.

I suppose I could have written twice as much as the 49,840 odd words that I have written in here if I had noted down every little incident that has happened. I have done what I can to make a brief account of the writeable things. The Air Force allows no diaries and so, even with this lot, I could be hamstrung! I have mentioned little about tactics, secret instruments used by either side, weapons, or to cut it short, anything that would be a really black, black. However such as it is, it should prove quite interesting if the need arises, or, for when I come home again even more so. After consultation here on a particular day, I am sure I shall be able to enlarge upon it in talk and explanation.

It's damned difficult sometimes, when things are moving quickly, or on leave, to keep it going. Any brevity that is obvious, is quite likely due to this. Apart from that I hate the war, and I find it hard to sit down and write all about it. I'd give anything to be home again. Let me say here and now that if anyone is keyed up and uneasy on ops NOT QUITE trembling, then it's me. I'm damned thankful to get down each time although I get a kick out of a good trip and to know that some more time may be cut off the length of this war, even if it's only a minute, by what I've helped to do. I'm darned if I know, but probably somewhere in here I have said shaky things or broken promises, indeed, anything! I don't know until I read it through. I think I can explain anything at all inside it though, that is something.

And now England. Poor England, so full of worry and trouble, bustle and noise, clouds and fog, laughter and joy, misery and sorrow — silly, wonderful, little, big Britain, what do I think of her at this time? Well, I'm still damned if I know. I don't think I'll ever know just what to think about it. Everybody who knows London, loves London so they say. Personally I dislike London yet I am always willing to give up a day of any leave to spend it in London. Perhaps this is because it's the only place in Britain I have yet discovered where things are anywhere near modern, not that they are here. Perhaps it's because it's the largest, and I am told, the most historic city in the world, or perhaps because the Boomerang Club is situated there. In the summer time I love the countryside. In the winter it is too cold, foggy and miserable to love anything except a huge fire. The BBC is dreadful — no opposition, of course. Some of the people are wizard half of the time and half of the people are a dead loss some of the time. So, to say I love England would be very wrong, but to say I am proud of her and what she has done would be very correct.

Life I have found here to be far easier to live than at home. Most married people are very happy regardless of their circumstances. The OK Jack, I'm alright, attitude is everywhere. People are content with very little, sometime, I would venture to say, they would be afraid to have more because tradition would not allow it. The force of tradition is terrific and therefore the like father, like son policy is very much the thing.

I love the very very English people — love that is, in perhaps the fascinated sense if there is one. I could sit and watch and listen to some old well-to-do family for hours or even days. In time I suppose I would get sick of it. I have been surprised to find so many of the young British people who have one aim — to leave England straight after the war to go to the Dominions and America. The war has opened the door to another room to them. They have never seen inside this room before, most of them have not wanted to, and now when they can see just a little through the doorway they look about and compare it with their lot. And some of them kick themselves for not having tried to open the door before. But how different is Scotland. I do like Scotland and its people. I love the Scottish countryside — and Edinburgh too.

September time. What would I do, or give, to see a wattle tree in blossom, the clear skies and sunshine, the open country stretching for miles, the gum trees — the twisted red gums or the tall ash of the forest, — a clear stream in the hills with all the ferns and greenery, the trout season has just opened too. My God! What shall I do after the war? This is the big question. It all depends I guess what the 'Pat situation' is like. Sometimes everything seems so futile but then when you look around at the wonderful and beautiful things in life, it's worth while climbing the ladder after all, no matter how high it is, or how long it takes.

Monday 18 September: Straight after lunch we walk to Hykham Station to catch our train to Nottingham where we change to the London train. We have to wait a short time before we can get into the Strand Palace Hotel so we pass the time in the Savoy Tavern. After getting our rooms we go down to Codger's Club, off Fleet St, for a few more. Then back to the Tavern and then bed. There are flying bombs tonight.

Tuesday 19 September: Before lunch Spanner, Geoff and I go down the Strand shopping. (I buy a watch, fountain pen and travelling bag.) We all have lunch at the Boomerang Club. Here we meet Chiefy White and Trevor Ramsay the only survivors from Rod's crew. They were shot down by a fighter near the Belgian frontier. Chiefy got out through a hole on the starboard side of the nose while the crate dived in flames from 15,000. They both evaded capture and were looked after by the FFI until our troops advanced into the area. Chiefy fought with the Marquis, killing several Huns at close quarters. He found their crashed A/C and helped bury the five others — or what they could find of them. Both are returning home.

Bill leaves for Oxford soon after lunch. We have a second lunch at the Trocadero — Salted Almond in Shaftsbury Av, near Piccadilly. In the evening we have a few sips at the Savoy Tavern and to finish, Spanner and I hail a taxi and go to Euston to catch our respective trains. I manage to get a seat and I spend a most uncomfortable night trying to sleep or read. Neither are at all successful. It's so stuffy too.

Wednesday 20 September: At about 0530 I tumble out at Carlisle and begin immediately to freeze. I walk around, having odd cups of tea, until the Edinburgh train comes in at about 0640. I am too tired and dirty-feeling to enjoy the border hill country as we pass through it, and eventually arrive at St Boswells where I manage to hire a car (Austin VIII) to 'Monteviot' estate. This time it only costs me 12/6 — astonishing! Well of course I receive the usual welcome of smiles, whisky and jumping dogs and at once I don't feel too bad. I have a meal and then a rest. After tea I sneak up the back way to the woods and shoot a couple of rabbits. On return I get back to old form with a supper of boiled eggs and Scottish shortbread before going to bed.

Saturday 23 September: I have been having a fine time as usual. The fishing situation is out, the water being very high and discoloured. On the other hand the shooting situation is admirable with the grouse and partridge seasons both open now. It is a bit wet underfoot now and the grass is very long and damp. Really there is too much cover for shooting, but the birds are plentiful and they give good sport. I have been eating like a king and never have I risen earlier than 1000. My thoughts have been miles away from war, except when I read the paper to find where the boys have been. (Yesterday afternoon I went to Hawick. This V-1 is proving a damned nuisance to all and sundry. I wonder what V-2 will be like.) Old Peter, the labrador, and I have had numerous happy wanderings in the woods over an endless thick carpet of brown leaves. Sometimes I have not taken a gun and simply wandered about in complete contentment. This is a wizard sort of rest. Again I thank my lucky stars that I have a place like this to come to, — and such lovely people. This afternoon I go to Jedburgh in the car with Mac and Euph. I do a spot of shopping and buy Pat shoes, of a most quaint type, that are being worn here now because of lack of leather. They have wooden soles. I get them more from the keepsake point of view. I also get her a scarf.

Euph takes me over the old Abbey. It is extremely historic, having been burnt down seven times by the English during the old Border Wars. I gather some stone from the cloister walls. Excavation is taking place still. I find it very interesting. Back at 'Woodside' we have a hasty meal before Mac and I go up the wood. It is too dark however to see much. We catch the ravens returning to their rookiers in the pines though, and manage to kill seven

between us. We have our supper and a game of Haymarket — which I
learn from the others.

Tuesday 26 September: Well, the time has come again for me to push
off. As usual I have had a wonderful time. Every single opportunity I have
had to go hunting I have taken. I feel 100% better for the exercise and
change. The weather has been wonderful considering the time of the year.
I pack up my things and Euph gives me 7 hard boiled eggs and some
tomatoes to put in too. They drive me down to the bus stop to catch the
1208 to Edinburgh. We have just got time to have a few words and away I
go. I enjoy the country scenery as we pass through it. Everything is bare of
course but quite pretty.

At Edinburgh I meet Bill and Margaret, his friend (whom he hopes to
marry) at the bus stop. We leave her after a while and go to the Grand Hotel
(where we are to stay) while I get rid of my bags. Then we go off hunting
souvenirs and antiques. I buy all manner of stuff and return to fill a butter
box with it (plus the things I bought in Jedburgh) for Pat. I take it to an
coin-monger's shop where the chap nails and wires it up for me. I then post
it, with much trouble — red tape and customs rot! In Princes Street I find
a pair of fifteen pound fifteen shilling diamond studded wings at a big
jeweller's store. I get them without hesitation as a Christmas present for Pat,
along with the five pound five shillings gold thistle brooch I got in Hawick.

We have tea at the Three Feathers, and then another one at some place in
Princes Street. Back at the 'pub' we have a few drinks before going to a
dance at the Locarno per tram. Here we have quite a fair time and afterwards
cart a pair o' wee lassies home (which, by good management, is just a short
step down the road!), then we catch the last train home and manage to get
a couple of drinks at the Hotel Residents' Bar. And so to bed.

Wednesday 27 September: Up early in order to catch our train going
South. We stand in a queue for almost an hour to get a seat. Margaret
comes to see Bill off. At length we are away and I see a tear in Marg's eye.
Travelling by train in war-time Britain is no joke, it's a positive nightmare
and by the time Bill and I get to Grantham we have not enough courage to
catch the connecting train to Lincoln so decide to take the bus. Again we
stand in a queue — this time we freeze. Here a bit of one two goes on as
there are some mischievous looking blondes awaiting departure in another
bus. It turns out quite amusing, for our bus, taking the same route, overhauls
and passes them, then slows down. They follow all the way until we are
some 5 mins out of Lincoln before alighting — damned poor show indeed.

From Lincoln we manage to catch a taxi to camp where we find the others already home. My God, W-Willie has gone! Well, I'm damned. F/O Hornibrook, an Aussie, took her to the Dortmund-Ems canal and is missing. F/Lt Stone and F/O Goodbrand, both RAF, are also missing from 61. 50 Squadron also have lost some crews since we have been away. This is indeed a blow. I expect we shall have to take any old kite until another W arrives for us — and there are some crates about. Willie, and the kangaroo I painted on her nose has gone for a burton. The whole business shakes me rigid. Pexton has taken over W/C of the Squadron as W/C Doubleday DSO, DFC is time and tour expired and is posted to 27 OTU Litchfield.

I go to bed thinking a lot, and in poor spirits.

Thursday 28 September: In the afternoon we go in G–George to pick up Y-Yoke which landed on 3 at Oulton in Norfolk. This is a 100 Gp airfield with RAF B-17s and B-24s. We collect the A/C and return to base, landing at about 1800. Tonight we do a little cooking in the hut and have a magnificent feed from our home parcels before turning in.

Saturday 30 September: S/L Hadden, a second tour bod, arrives to take the position of B FLT Commander. He seems a bull'oish but harmless old bloke with all the OTU red tape still hanging about his shoulders. We'll train 'im! In the afternoon we go to Wigsley on an NRF. Here I invite F/O Scott DFC, one of my old instructors to our Mess Party which is to come off during the moon period sometime. After tea Geoff, Bill, Jack and I go across to the Fox and Hounds for a few pints. We have cheese sandwiches on the house.

Wednesday 4 October: In the afternoon when I am feeling better, we do a low level X-country. (Base – Kings Lynn – Spalding – Sleaford – Base. Round twice.) We have a fine look at Spanner's home at Kings Lynn and over the Wash we shoot up a few seals that are lying out on the sand-banks. A plover gets in our way and crashes straight through the B/A's window to scatter itself all over the B/A himself, much to Darkie's wrath, and our amusement. Afterwards we do some A/S/F and Bill shoots the starboard 1196 radio aerial away! Having wrecked old X enough by this I turn for base and land successfully. I let Jock do some flying on the way home.

Thursday 5 October: War. Target Wilhelmshaven. 12 x 1000, 2 x 500 Docks and U-Boat pens. Operate in daylight! Mustang escort.

Ops meal is at 0230. Eventually after one false start we get weaving. I am Deputy NO 2 to W/C Pexton. We pick up our Mustang escort at position X (Catfoss) and proceed. We stray to port and go very close to Heligoland where a heavy barrage greets us. Low st. cu. about 6/10 ths covers the target. H2S A/C run up OK and I bomb when they do. Heavy, but inaccurate predicted flak comes up, but I see no fighters. Some A/C bomb farms and small villages on the way out across the coast. I wish I still had mine for there are wizard targets — even a small vessel lying close to the shore. Only one bomber is missing on return. We cook ourselves some supper.

Friday 6 October: War. Target Bremen. 16 cans. Night fire raid. The new P-Peter has arrived and we are to take it to war tonight. All goes OK until we are well out across the North Sea at about 2000' when the rear turret becomes U/S. Geoff, Spanner and Bill work for half an hour to fix it, but their attempts are in vain. I therefore return to base, jettisoning down to 56, 65m NE of Skegness, much to the disappointment of our 2nd Dickie, F/O Cadman. He seems a very nice chap indeed and I should like to have taken him along to break the duck. The risk is too great, however, to chance 7 lives as well as my own. We land a little heavily due to an unexpected slow running on this A/C. Just as we pass F/C on the perimeter track, the port tyre blows out so we leave the old thing there. Well, we have joined the Boomerang Club! They say you never finish a tour without a boomerang in your log book, so this is something. This new A/C seems a wizard kite and the ground crew also appear to be good types. Those we had on W were bang on chaps all round especially Jimmy Meuse. I still have that funny worried sort of feeling inside me. I'm damned if I want to die yet. Life is too much worth while to say goodbye to it early in the piece. I put a successful tour down to 80% good management and skill, and 20% luck. You must have the luck part of it though, that is certain. How you miss a load of incendiaries or odd cookies at night, I'm damned if I know. I'm going to be grey haired soon I reckon.

Saturday 7 October: War. Target Flushing. 14 x 1000. ½ hour delay. Sea wall. Daylight operation. Spits escort.

On T/O the front hatch blows up. It's a bit of a shaky do while Darkie tries to get it back on. I make him put on his chute in case he falls out, which he almost does, only Spanner is holding him. At length anyway they close it. We do two runs over the A/P, 7 bombs at a time. Flak is not too bad. It seems a good prang. Tonight all of us except Darkie and Bill go down to the Fox and Hounds for a pint or two.

Wednesday 11 October: War. Target Flushing. 14 x 1000 Gun positions in concrete emplacements. Daylight. 100 Gp Spit and Typhoon escort. B/H 6,500'.

We do a dummy run because of cloud, but on the second run we hit it

Taking a break, Santa Fe Rail Road.

Times Square, New York, 1943.

Lancaster bombers head across the Channel near Brighton at dusk.

Author and Mac Kennedy outside a Nissen hut at Church Lawford.

Off duty haunts: Above Olde Bull Inn, Wooton Wawan. Below Alfriston – where King Alfred burnt the cakes!

Sir Reginald Blaker's home, Balcombe, Sussex.

Darkie Mayall at Silverstone.

Author at Bayworth Corner, Oxfordshire.

Geoff Allen in his turret.

Bill Jackman in his turret (mid-upper).

Our Wellington in dispersal bay, Turweston.

Wellington crew left to right: Bill Jackman (mid upper gunner), Des Murray (navigator), Ron 'Darkie' Mayall (bomb aimer), unnamed flight mechanic, Jock Gardner (radio operator/air gunner) and Geoff Allen (rear gunner).

Author looks down almost nine metres from Stirling cockpit.

Typhoon (note invasion stripes).

Hurricane fighter-bomber.

D-Day softening-up aircraft included the rocket-firing Mosquito.

Woodside — the gamekeeper's cottage on the Earl of Ancrum's estate.

Tom Maclean, the Monteviot Estate gamekeeper and my host when in Scotland.

Ops planning at Skellinthorpe base. Left to right S/L Stubbs, DFC, RAF, G/C Jefferson, RAF, S/L Quinn, DFC, RAF, W/C Doubleday, DSO, DFC, RAAF.

Bombing up S-Sugar — a 61 Squadron Lancaster.

Lancaster crew. Left to right Bill, Geoff, Darkie, Spanner, self, Jock. Absent Navigator, Des.

Author at cockpit window.

Des Murray beside his Gee screen.

P-Peter repalced our first Lancaster W-Willie — lost in September 1944 on a Dortmund-Ems canal raid.

Total destruction after a fire raid burnt out Darmstadt city, Monday 11 September 1944.

Le Havre, 10 September 1944. Very accurate daylight bombing was developed by 5 Group Lancasters.

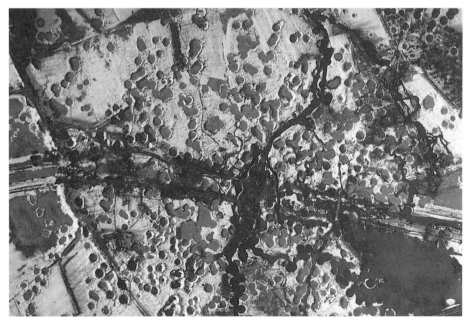

Dortmund-Ems canal breached again. Note bomb craters in snow.

V-1 missiles produced great horizontal blast and damage. The V-2 rocket had less horizontal blast but great penetration. Note building fallen into crater.

Author takes his last flight in England over snow-covered Somerset in a Beaufighter

smack on. The gunners see the bombs explode across the target. However we have two hang-ups and I get Darkie to aim at some slit trenches and M/T facilities at the NW tip of Walcheren Is. I do two runs for him here too. They overshoot slightly, but one lands on the road near Huns. The weather for return is poor, and makes flying unpleasant. Drift is bad on landing.

Saturday 14 October: The boys go to Brunswick tonight, on a fire raid. F/O Hoad is missing on return. He had F/O Cadman with him as 2nd Dickie. I wish doubly now that I had taken him to Bremen successfully. He was such a decent sort of chap. (A/C Y-Yoke.) The boys report many large fires on return — good show. F/O Collins lands at Woodbridge with no ASI.

Sunday 15 October: This afternoon I take P to Woodbridge to pick up Collins and crew. We return individually however as his A/C is serviceable when I get there. In the evening I write home and to Pat.

Monday 16 October: Stand by — Target Munchen Gladback in the Rhur. Weather scrubs it, or somebody talked.

Tuesday 17 October: War. Target Hanover — scrubbed, bad weather again.

Thursday 19 October: War. Target Nuremburg. 'Cookie' and J type clusters. Night show, of course. Fire raid on city centre. On attack 97 A/C are lost.

All goes well on the way there. We see a raid going on at Stuttgart by 1 & 3 Gps as we pass it. A couple of crates go down while I look that way. We are a few minutes late in bombing (15,000') and are at the lowest height. Just after we drop our load — not more than 15 secs after either, we are predicted and hit by heavy flak. The A/C goes into a violent turn to starboard and loses height. This is the way we are supposed to turn anyway so I let it go. I find that the bomb doors will not close even by the emergency system and that the DR compass is U/S. By this time the A/C flies OK so I proceed to lose height down to 9 thou into st. cloud where I stay. Jock reports that hyd. fluid and petrol is all over the place aft and there are many holes torn in the fuselage. Everyone is unhurt luckily. I cannot maintain a good speed with the bomb doors open and we become a straggler 25 minutes late at the second T/P. 'Window', coming in through the holes in the floor tends to short Jock's acks, so Spanner takes it off by hand although sparks and flame keep appearing. We begin to ice up and I cannot climb.

Chunks of ice crash through the perspex off the airscrews, and Spanner is struck in the face. We are losing fuel from the port No. 1 tank. Jock is so cold that he cannot move and remains huddled on the floor. I manage to gain a little height, almost stalling and stay in and out of cloud. Eventually I see the French coast and we a/c immediately for Woodbridge and I hope to God we make it. On arrival there I find the R/T is U/S so use the Aldis for permission to pancake. We pull the bottle and land with bomb doors open and half flap at 135 mph. I now find that the tail wheel is missing, but I don't give a damn because we're down and alive! (The old crate is full of holes, petrol is pouring out of her when we land and the fuselage is broken close to the mid upper turret, where there is a huge hole. Some pieces of flak went darned near some of the chaps — Darkie and Bill especially — very lucky). After interrogation, a meal and a medical check I go to bed.

Friday 20 October: Eventually Air Crew Reception tell me that nobody is coming from base today to get us because of bad weather. So dammit, we are glad to be alive, so what? So we catch a transport to Woodbridge village and from there we catch a train to Ipswich (1/7d. ½ ticket). We look like six penneth of God help us as we stop off the train in flying kit, just as we stepped out of the crate. I have a battle dress on and Pat's blue scarf and no hat — it's raining like hell too! We check in at the Great White Horse Hotel, with a little bit of trouble, and have a clean up and shave with a bare blade. Anyway I go to bed after a most amusing and happy night, and, I believe some cheese sandwiches washed down with brandy.

Saturday 21 October: We return to Woodbridge very shakily this morning. At about 1500 F/O Hill RCAF arrives to take us back to base. I travel as Rear Gunner and have some fun in the rear turret. I should hate to be one by trade, there is such a feeling of detachment about the whole affair.

I write home and to Pat tonight.

Monday 23 October: We get a brand new plane from the factory.

Tuesday 24 October: In the afternoon we go down to Church Lawford for a visit. The vis. is duff but we get in OK after a while, only just though. I see, and stagger, my old BAT instructor F/S, now W/O Topley, also a few of the other people I knew while I was there. It is quite amusing for, when we land, the ambulance, plus doctor and fire engine, turn out to meet us plus all the bods on the station. They think we are back from ops, and in trouble. Darkie drops off here as he is going home for a night — crafty devil — he's in love though! Back at base vis. is very duff, but I get in OK and am quite pleased with myself. Old S/L Blackmore in flying control congratulates me on R/T. Tonight we take the ground staff down to the Plough for a sip or two. They, and we, have a very satisfactory trip.

Wednesday 25 October: War. Target Flushing. 14 x 1000 Gun positions that are worrying the Canadian troops on the mainland. Daylight operation from 4–5 thou.

Things are unsatisfactory from the start with low cloud and rain. However we reach the target finally at about 4 thou. Flak is heavy and accurate. I see one A/C burning on the ground. On the run up my starboard aileron is shot away and the A/C holed in other places. It is very difficult to control and so I am forced to jettison the load. Another A/C goes down over the target and I narrowly miss collision with two other Lancs on a reciprocal heading. It is a shambles of an attack. Base is fit on return and we get in OK. Hugh Horsley has 179 holes in his crate! Old Si Borsht from Waddo is missing, plus 3 others from there. I learn later on down at the Plough. Bardney lost 4 crates too.

Saturday 28 October: War. Target Bergen. U–Boat pens. 10 x 1000 HE/SAP. Night attack 11,000 ft B/H.

We have F/O Ainsworth as 2nd Dickie, a small fellow with a nice disposition. The target is cloud covered and we ice up heavily at 12,000'. I dive across the area at 300 through predicted flak. The collision risk is very grave so I turn out across the North Sea at 5000 ft still in cloud and hail. We are diverted to Leckinfield so I jettison completely. On arrival at this station I find cloud below me at 600'. An A/C collides with a factory chimney on my starboard bow down so I climb quickly to 1500 and proceed to some Sandra lights. This is Pocklington, where after an overshoot I land. Oodles more A/C come in here. After interrogation and a meal I go to sleep in the Officers' Mess beside a poor fire. A very shaky do this with plenty of panic attached to it — should have been scrubbed.

Sunday 29 October: After refuelling we T/O and return to base — first off and first back home. I am very tired having had little sleep, after a particularly nasty flight so I go straight to my bed quite done in and feeling a bit dizzy. Tomorrow we are due to go on leave so I have no worries, only pleasures to dream about.

Monday 30 October: This morning I get up early, pack, see the Adj and go to Waddo for some money. Bill, Des, Geoff, Jock, Stewart (Bill's brother, who has been staying here for a short while) and I catch the 1350 London train. The journey is, of course, unbearable and utterly cheesing. Bill and I get into the Strand Palace without delay or trouble, while the others have to wait a while. We go to the Boomerang Club first where I see a few fellows I know. Then we go to the Savoy Tavern and begin a night's solid drinking at various pubs while V-1 passes overhead and explodes round about. Bill and I finish up together and have supper somewhere down in Fleet St!

To bed — and the 'all clear' goes off.

Tuesday 31 October: I rise at about 10 am and go to the Boomer for breakfast. Jock, Des and Geoff go to have a look around St Paul's, Westminster and other places of note, which they have not been able to visit as yet. I go up to Overseas HQ and get some mail. There are some interesting objects in the lobby which originally belonged to the GAF. I also buy a couple of maps of NE France and Southern Germany. From here we walk down to the Overseas Club. This is my first visit here and I find it an old but attractive place with a large bar, dance floor and dining rooms. I am told that members can stay here. Anyway we have some beer before we give the dance a go. Bill leaves at about 2200 to catch his train to Edinburgh.

Well old Ike and his Armies in France have certainly shaken things up in the past few months. They have shaken and inspired me I know, but I don't think he'll go much further now for a while. They'll have to clear Antwerp port for supplies first. Apart from that Jerry is still very much alive, contrary to the belief of many blind people, and he will not allow us into the Reich without a terrific last effort. My guess is that the Rhine will stop us until the Spring or the Summer of 1945.

Friday 3 November: Tonight I go to the Overseas Club once more and I meet a WAAF named Joan Andrews. She, her friend Betty, and a Yank and I go to some Chinese place, near Piccadilly, for some supper. We take them to Oxford Circus tube station and say g'night. I am going to meet Joan tomorrow night.

Saturday 4 November: Joan and I go to the Hungaria in St James for dinner and stay there all the evening although I have some tickets for the Carlton. We have an extremely nice meal. The atmosphere here is bang on too, I understand that it was a house for the nobility before the war. Even now only officers in the Services are admitted. After dinner down below in the lounge bar I get the gen on Joan — a most interesting story, and of course I think I should do something about it all. It appears that she was at school when war broke out, like myself, and in the panic of call up she was drafted to Accounts Section, Balloon Command HQ to do her damnedest. And there she has been against her will amongst the best chaircrew ever since — poor girl!

She met this American type, who succeeded in sweeping her away. So on November 23rd they were to be wed, begad. However, (through obscure channels) she finds that he is already married and of course scrubs him, much to his anger which he shows in a most vulgar and unmanly fashion — to wit, a cad! She is most depressed and I can well understand it, because she was in earnest. (She has had 7 proposals, including this one!) To cut a long story short she has been led up the garden path a long way, being a complete sucker, and now, after the bottom has fallen out of it, she considers the whole affair a definite dead loss, and wants to forget it all smartly. Eventually I put her on the last train to Stanmore and walk back up the Strand from Trafalgar Square to the Hotel, where I have a couple of drinks and sandwiches before going to bed. During the night I hear V-1.

Monday 6 November: I add to my collection of maps, and get some weeds from HQ this morning after a late breakfast. I have found a wizard little cafe not far from the Strand where they turn on a bang on meal, always with tomatoes, and I have been patronising them there a great deal.

Geoff and I have lunch at a lobster shop in the Strand (15/-) and buy one to take away with us (another 15/-).

Tuesday 7 November: At 1000 hrs I get up and have the old bath. Then Geoff and I go to the Boomer for lunch. He rings Jock up, who is down at Bexley.

I meet Joan at 1200 and have late lunch at the Chicken Inn. Later on we go back to the Strand where we see Jock and Geoff for a few minutes. At 1830 Joan and I go to Oxford Circus to meet two of her friends F/Lt Ken Roost and his fiancee Edna somebody. We have dinner at Coles, near Baker Street tube, after which we have a few sips round about. I go out to Stanmore with them and catch the last train back to Trafalgar Square. It is raining like hell all the time, and, while walking up to the hotel I get wet to the skin. Ken, a GAF radar wodda, is a very decent fellow indeed, who expects to go to Holland re same shortly. He and I get on very well.

No buzz-bombs tonight.

Thursday 9 November: We catch a train which goes fine until almost into Grantham when, due to a prang ahead, we are delayed an hour and a half! Gawd, what a dump of a place, this England. At length we reach Lincoln and manage to secure a taxi which takes us to the railway gates. I call in at the mess and get my mail. There is some from Pat which makes me very happy after such a stinking trip up. She's tops. Now, if she was here, she'd shake the living daylights out of all these people over here. Somebody pinches my gloves while I am in beside the fire reading my mail. It's after 1 am too!

I discover that F/O McLaughton is missing from a raid on Dusseldorf and that F/O Macfarland shot down a JU88 and a Jet A/C on the same attack. They have operated very little in our absence, due to bad weather. They have been briefed a lot though. They did a daylight to Homburg in the Rhur.

Saturday 11 November: The boys go to Harburg, near Hamburg, to bash synthetic oil plants and the town.

F/O Hill is attacked by a JU88 and is lucky to get back at all, due to extensive damage on all port surfaces. He is hit by flak too. S-Sugar is therefore cat AC. He is a bit of a straight and level type. I go out and have a look at the A/C as soon as he has landed.

Monday 13 November: I buy a little 1928 Morris Minor for fifteen pounds. With a bit of work Spanner and I reckon we can get her pretty well bang on. Tonight we take it, with five in it, to the Fox and Hounds for a drink or two. We have an excellent time, of course.

Wednesday 15 November: In a snow storm a 15 Cwt. Comer runs into Ernie Vale and I in the car. The right hand wheel and mud guard are bent a bit, also the axle and track rod. We set about fixing it up. With the aid of M/T and station workshops we get it right at 6.30 pm. She has a violent swing to port though — poor show.

Thursday 16 November: War. Target Duren. B/H 8000 ft force 1150. Daylight, but we are almost scrubbed from the battle order soon after briefing as the W/C has to go along. We see plenty of flak but no fighters, all 61 return. Some are lost from other bases. Target totally wiped out. Also Julich.

We spend our time working on the car at night.

Monday 20 November: Petrol load reduced from 2154 to 1500 and 13 x 1000 replace the 1 x 4000 and 9 x J clusters. However the op is scrubbed at 1630. Briefing was to begin at 2100! I write letters tonight. Today another letter from Stanmore!

Tuesday 21 November: Flight Leut today. F/Lt! War. Target Ladbergen — Dortmund Ems canal. 13 x 1000 Night time. H-Hour put back 3 hours. B/H 12 lowest 2!

We have a darned good trip. All Belgium is lit up as we pass over it. We bomb from 5/5 after a drop from 12 because of cloud (st. cu.) over target. I can see the canal plainly on the run up. There is another attack by the Gp further up towards Munster tonight. Both attacks go off OK. On the way home there are plenty of fighter flares and a rising moon. I see only one A/C shot down myself. The Cont. becomes coned!

Wednesday 22 November: War. Target Trondheim U-Boat pens. 9 x 1000 SAP/HE and full tanks. 11 thou B/H.

We are early at target so dogleg. Hun is too clever and puts up a smoke screen with small M/Bs in the harbour. The Controller decides to A/M because of risk of damage to Norwegian people. I jettison just off the coast. The way home is as bad as the way out was with frontal cloud from 1500' to 20,000', I fly back across the North Sea at about 800 ft. Due to fuel shortage I a/c Peterhead and land at 0132. After interrogation and a wizard meal we go to bed. The six wind finding Mosquito XUs land here — or rather five, as one ditched through lack of fuel. The winds were extraordinarily strong tonight. We had a ground speed of only 158 tonight on return.

Thursday 23 November: We try to get off at about noon today to return to base, but the SI is U/S. Spanner and I refuel to 1200 gals however. This is a long range escort P-51 airfield with mostly Polish pilots. Am I ever green with envy! They are a lovely crate. In the evening we catch a bus into the town of Peterhead where we go to a picture. It is surprisingly warm up here in Scotland — the wind is a bit chilly at times though.

Friday 24 November: We get off at about 1300. On the way down (after shooting the joint up) I find 'Monteviot' and circle it very low. The C/B is only 2,000 and I am not happy because of high ground so I climb to 4,000 to return. At base C/B is 400–500 ft so I do a split-oit circuit at about 200 ft. On the deck I find a war on with 2154 and 'Cookie' and clusters. I go to the W/C and tell him the crew is far to weary to fly so we are scrubbed. The target turns out to be Breslau! But after briefing it is scrubbed. I go to bed early. There was snow on the Border Hills. F/O James is missing from Trondheim. I thought he'd go.

Saturday 25 November: Damned near bust the car up today on the Waddo hill on return from getting some money. We end up between a fence, lamp post and car. Two old women nearly have kittens at the sight of it. We leave the car at a garage in Lincoln quite out of petrol and come home by taxi after a meal at the Albion.

Sunday 26 November: We have our first heavy frost this morning. Boy! is it cold.

War. Target Munich. 'Cookie' and clusters. Full tanks. Attack at night. Route takes us over the Alps.

All goes well until I am almost to the wagon for T/O when a fire develops in the rear turret due to fusing of gun-heaters. I taxi off port and await electricians. They say the A/Hs are U/S and there is a short up as far as the Elsan. They mess about trying to fix it until after last TOTA so I, as Captain, decide not to T/O late with a queer A/C on a 10½ hour trip. I don't know whether the crew are pleased with my action or not, but what I say goes in any case — never take more chances than necessary, that's me.

There are 3 Boomerangs from 61 tonight.

Thursday 30 November: This afternoon I take a big step and take P-Peter with two of our ground crew, across to Candover in Stropshire, to see Snake. On the way I find the crater where the huge explosion took place a day or two ago, killing about 205 people and demolishing two complete villages. It is an awful sight to see in England but a common one for the other side. It was an RAF bomb dump for 'cookies'. About 4,000 tons went up. The 'quake' shook Birmingham, Manchester, Sheffield, Shrewsbury and many other places within a 70 mile radius. It occurred near Burton-on-Trent.

I find Snake at Candover OK, and we are very pleased to see each other. This is a satellite of Fern Hill with Master IIIs. A Spit XIV drops in while we are there. (This is the first four engined A/C to land here up to date and the old F/C wadda is like a hairy goat with pleasure when I sign in.) I show Snake the works of the Lanc. It shakes him a bit with its size I reckon! I stay just over an hour before returning. I am so glad to have seen the old reptile again. My God I'm yearning to get weaving up amongst the streams with him after the show. He seems pretty keen on a girl from Huddersfield. Maybe there is going to be English blood in the family. Never mind so long as she can cook and get on with Pat OK, I can see no problem in it. If he took her home he'd certainly be doing her a good turn getting her out of this misery land. Proud of him!

Vis is duff at base on return. I let Jock fly for a while on the way home. The erks enjoy their ride very much. Gunners fire guns.

Monday 4 December: War. Target Heilbronn. 18 x J clusters. Rail junction and town, vital to the enemy. B/H 13,850'. Operate at night.

This is a very fine war. We have a good trip all the way round. It is a little twitchy though — 1 & 3 Gps attack Karlsruhe at the same H-Hour. 17

A/C are lost from Command and 15 are on Hielbronn! 190s, 88s and 109s all up in strength. It is a wizard prang the entire target area is devastated by HE and fire bombs. Flak is light. Icing heavy. All 61 return. F/O Collins spends his 21st birthday over the target! He has 3 combats with an 88 in addition to a complete hang up. They manage to jettison the 'cookie' manually. Well, this leaves one trip to go. I shan't say any more. A man has got to be darned unlucky to go on his last trip — let's leave it at that just now.

Wednesday 6 December: War. Target Giessen. 18 x J clusters. Rail junction. Night trip. B/H 10,850. Into the night fighter land.

The weather is the worst thing on the way. Over England I fly at about 1000 ft I hold this across and into France. At about 3° E I climb to 3 soon after up to B/H getting iced up into the bargain. We bomb a bit late. (Jock puts on a show when the I/C goes haywire with his, 'Ha ha hello' business). It appears a good prang. I see air to air firing and one A/C on fire. Also a load of incendiaries jettisoned on the way out of the target. Over Belgium on return we run into electrical storms with hail and sleet. I fly at about 1000 again with nav lights on (not lower, because A/C have been shot down for V-1 because of them). Flying becomes very unpleasant. However, over the channel it breaks up, and England is clear.

Back at base we are congratulated no end, and told we are the first crew to finish on a P for 18 months! A public relations wodda asks me many questions for the Australian newspapers, especially Melbourne papers. Geoff pulls his chute to see if it would have worked! It does. Darkie tells me how the B/S went U/S and he used his fingers! — Crafty lad, the old Dark. Everybody is very happy. I myself feel a greater feeling of relief than I have ever felt. I may do another tour before I'm finished, against the Japanese, but let that come when it's due. Right now I feel bang on. I have a meal and go off to bed finding no trouble going to sleep.

Thursday 7 December: Tonight we take the ground staff out for a big party across to the Bridge Hotel, Saxilby. Sixteen of us go altogether (five going in my little car). It is awfully cold, but we soon get warmed up with a couple under the belt. Certainly without these fellows we could never have dropped 420,000 lbs odd of stuff on the Hun. The meal is magnificent and the boys thoroughly enjoy themselves. There are speeches all round. (I explain how I consider I have not given Darkie quite as fair a go as I might have.) At the end of the evening we all have on different tunics — I am an LAC! We are all quite happy. I drive home OK. Jock however, on his bike ends up in a canal and arrives back in a very wet state.

Friday 8 December: I go to Waddo and collect some money in the morning and also wire the Strand Palace re a room. I hear that Don Smith is missing on Dusseldorf. Bill and Geoff set off to Leicester before lunch and I follow up after, having mended my trousers, and arrive at the Grand Hotel at about 2000 hrs. The others arrive (all except Darkie) and after booking in we drink in Simon's Bar until it closes when we go to The Swan with Two Necks to finish up. We're on leave again, but this is a special leave — it's finishing leave! Boy are we going to have a time. I get pretty tight tonight.

Sunday 10 December: When I get up Bill and Geoff have already left for their respective destinations (Edinburgh and Liverpool). Jock and I leave for London at 1027. Des comes to the station with us, as his train to Birmingham goes at 1113. We arrive in London after a wretched journey and to make it worse, it's raining hard. We manage to get a taxi to the Strand Palace, and get a double room. We then go to the Boomerang Club for tea. Here I meet a few of the boys. Harry Redwood (463), Jock Lee (from school who tells me that Nick Martin is over here) and Ferdie McNicol is an instructor at home. (BAGS I believe), Mickey Clarke, and some others. I ring Joan up and arrange to meet her at 1900 at Oxford Circus. Before going there I have a few drinks with Jock at the Savoy Tavern. He is going on down to Bexley tomorrow. Joan and I have a quiet but interesting evening. I put her on the last train for Stanmore. There's nothing like a little feminine company, like salt or water, it is a necessity of life.

Wednesday 13 December: After a trip to Trafalgar Square tube I have some breakfast and ring up Jock. He suggests I come down. This I do in very weary form, and on arrival they all nearly drop dead. The people that he stays with are very nice types and I am at once given a huge lunch. The Crossed Keys is about 20 yds away, just across the road, and the Three Blackbirds is not much further away. I can understand why Jock is so much at home down here! Later in the afternoon Jock and I toddle down the road in the most awful fog I have ever seen, to see the show 'For Whom the Bell Tolls' at the Plaza. The fog is a dirty brown colour. On the way home it is dark and the fog is worse. It takes us about an hour to make our way half a mile. All the buses and trains have been halted. What a country! We have tea and then go across to the pub for a while, returning with six quart bottles.

V-1 and V-2 are very common noises down here. I noticed considerable damage to houses on the way down in the train. Frank is a warden, and he tells me many astonishing tales about these latest weapons used by the Hun.

V-1 is definitely the worst of the two. Its arrival and blast effect are much more spectacular and shaking. The fog clears enough for me to catch a train at 12.50 (after waiting since 10.57 on a freezingly cold platform with no coat). I get to Charing Cross at 0115 and go immediately to bed.

Saturday 16 December: This evening a V-2 explodes very nearby. This damned business is a poor show, he's doing no military damage at all, but simply killing civilians like flies and scaring others almost out of their wits, not to mention the damage to residential areas. All I hope is that my bombs didn't all kill outright those they fell upon, but caused suffering, pain and shock, before death! We have dinner at the Salted Almond and end up at the Savoy Tavern before a visit to the Strand. Here the finishing touches are put on it as a V-2 lands outside Charing Cross tube doing much damage.

Sunday 17 December: I get up at about 1130, take the old bath of course, have breakfast down the road at a cafe in the Strand. Meet Jock for lunch at 1315 but he doesn't arrive until 1435. Cheesed to hell and demand an explanation. He missed his train! Women! Lunch is just managed to be got at the Strand Grill Room, after which we see a newsreel. We collect our things and taxi to Kings Cross for our Lincoln train. I shudder to think of the trip ahead.

Poor Joan is a bit keen I'm afraid, but there's no show here. I wish I could get home to a real girl. There are no substitutes in the world for Pat, I'm quite definite about that. But I've grown really fond of Joan. She's a close second and had I never known Pat, who knows? Bill is pretty sure to cart Margaret back home. This is a pretty grim moment which I shall never forget and I admit I lose part of my heart at Kings Cross. Joan looks so lovely in her grey WAAF uniform with her big sad brown eyes — but Pat has brown eyes too! After a tearful kiss we're off reaching Lincoln late, feeling dirty and tired. While waiting the 1½ hours at the taxi place, we are joined by Bill who comes home with us. Here at camp is a stack of mail for me — wizard (and I don't lose my gloves).

Well that's that lot finished. It has been a good leave. Perhaps I should have gone to Scotland, I don't know. I love the bush — any bush. I shall go there when the trout season opens again no doubt. It would certainly save money, I managed to spend about fifty pounds this leave. I have got something to show for it though, including another of Frank Wootton's famous paintings. Life is so carefree over here for me. I am far from home and it's easy to become lonely. It doesn't matter who you're with, or where you are, there's no place like home. The day I landed over here, I wanted to go back again. That's over 15 months ago now and I simply do the first thing that comes into my head. Nobody knows me, and I'm not keen to be known by many of these people. One thing I am proud of is the name I wear on my shoulder. I should never do anything to dishonour or let that name down. Australia is the only country in the world for me, she's tops.

Monday 18 December: Last night the chaps went to Munich again. F/O Newland, RCAF, is missing. I thought he'd go sooner or later. Tonight there is a war. Target Gydnia — shipping in the dock area (9 of Germany's remaining warships are there including 'Lutzow', 'Prinz Eugen', 'Gneisenau', 'Hipper' and others. Bill goes along as M/U to F/O Souter, on his last trip, and we see him off. Good luck Bill, I'd hate to see you go now after doing so many with us. Jock is posted to Kinningley!

Wednesday 20 December: Geoff has made a new water jacket cover for the car. This morning we fill up with 100 octane plus hydraulic oil. She belches smoke but goes.

We take some photos at the crate later and then I see S/L Hadden and F/Lt Glover re the gunner's commissions. I write home. In the evening all of us except Darkie go to the Plough and the Fox and Hounds.

Thursday 21 December: I drive the car to Waddo to get some money and take Geoff along too. On return we get a puncture. Tonight Des, Geoff and I set out for the 'Parklands' but half way get a blow-out! We leave the damned thing and walk there, drink, and walk home plus chips under each arm in the drizzling rain. I'm cheesed off — going to bed. Damn!! Spanner is posted to 5 LFS Syerston, much to his dislike.

Friday 22 December: Spanner and Jock leave. We collect the car. It's as cold as hell with an awful frost today. No sun. No warmth. No love. No nothing!

Saturday 23 December: Another frost and I'm miserably cold all day doing nothing, but sit by a fire after getting up at about 1230. I do some painting for S/O Brian. Tonight Bill, Geoff and I set out in the car to the Plough, via Thorpe-on-the-Hill and the Fox and Hounds. The boys went to Polentz (oil refineries near Stettin) the other night, being diverted to Dice and Bamph. They are just returning now, with a C/B of some 400–500'. There are some shaky do's as we drive around inside the Drem.

Last night V-1 was fired against Northern England for the first time. We hear them here but none fall on us.

Sunday 24 December: <u>XMAS EVE</u> — <u>1944</u>! Bill and Geoff pull me out of bed to go and get W/C Pexton to interview them regarding their commissions. I find him in good spirits and he sees them without any bother on the spot. (There is an awful frost today.) After lunch F/Lt Cree, F/O Hayley, F/O Friend, F/O Collins, F/Lt Burns, F/O Lushey and myself go in two cars on a pub crawl taking in Lincoln itself. We begin the evenings celebrations now and do rather well. I manage to lose my gloves. On return we continue with our private stock until it is time to get dressed for the party in the Mess. This I cannot remember very much about, except that it is a very fine show indeed. After tea three carloads begin at the Plough, returning to the Mess before supper is served. I tee a sort up for the W/C. I really have a whale of a time. Everybody is happy for a change, especially F/Lt Doc, F/Lt Hill, F/O Friend and others. I get home at about 0400.

Monday 25 December: <u>CHRISTMAS DAY</u>! Talk about a white Xmas — today the frost is terrific and crowns all frosts I have ever witnessed, this year, or last. Everything is white. The trees are coated in inches of ice. There is fog and mist too to cap things off. It's too cold to explain. As Nels Hill says, 'You just gotter keep tight to forget it!'. All the car radiators are frozen solid. Bottles of ink and hair oil inside also solidified. I'm just chilled to the bone and absolutely cheesed — I wanna go home! About midday the W/C grabs me in the Mess where all NCOs are invited this morning, and drives into Lincoln to look for the piece I teed up for him last night. Of course we must pick up Hugh Horsley on his way home and we end up in the Albion, where we find F/Os Mills and Atkinson plus wives, also F/Lt Bartlett and his wife and little son (she's wizard). We come back first in time to serve in the Airmen's Mess. I serve my ground staff first, of course. After this we go to the Sgt's Mess to serve, where I find Bill and Geoff in high spirits. They starve us till 1845 when we eat. The dinner is bang on but it's darned cold sitting. The G/C takes an awful time to rise. Another quite passable Xmas has had it then. I think last year's was a little better than this. My happiest thought at this time is that I am still alive — tour expired.

Thursday 28 December: Bill flies with F/Lt Boon tonight to Verle Bay in Oslo Fijord to attack Nazi shipping. Good luck son. I go to Flight Planning Conference to get the gen before he goes. We get our photos today that we had taken out at the kite.

Saturday 30 December: Bill goes with S/L Hawsley to Houffalize, near Bastogne to attack troop concentrations and arms dumps to weaken Rundstedt's salient. (4½ miles NNE of Bastogne.) I go to Flight Planning. H-Hour is put back from 2300 to 0500 because of weather. I don't think they'll go, but they do. I hear them T/O while I'm in bed. Good old Bill.

Geoff came to briefing with me. He had never, of course, been at a Captain's briefing before.

Sunday 31 December: <u>NEW</u> <u>YEAR'S EVE</u>! F/Lt Paul Crampton DFM and Spam is missing. He is a second tour bod, and last night he had a war correspondent flying with him. I had a funny feeling he'd go, and when I mention it to Ernie Vale, one of Paul's best friends he agrees with me. Lately he hasn't been home to see his wife at all. He's been hanging around with S/O Nigel — damned poor show. Since I have been here I have noticed a marked drop in his appearance. Of late he has looked like a scarecrow. Even so he was a good pilot and I expect something unlucky happened to bring him down. As the target was very near American troops, there is a very good chance that they have come down in friendly territory. I hope they are safe anyway.

Monday 1 January: <u>1945</u>! Dixie arrives back at about 0930 quite well away — been cooking eggs for the boys. Later they take off for the Dortmund Ems canal. A 50 OTU crate prangs on the runway with 14 x 1000 delays on. For an hour we await the bang in the shelters but nothing goes off. 7 A/C are prevented from T/O. Later still however the rest T/O for an attack on another part of the canal (12 miles north). The first lot were diverted to Coningsby on return. All 61 are down OK, two are on 3 engines.

The USAAF attack Germany for the 10th successive day. Targets today are an oil centre near Brunswick and a rail yard near Coblenz. Yesterday saw 3000 heavy bombers operate from this country — not a bad effort. During the foggy month of December the RAF alone dropped approximately 50,000 tons on the Hun. This morning the GAF made a determined effort to strafe our forward airfields near the push. First counts suggest he lost 125 A/C out of an attacking force of some 300. This is a darned good effort by the fighter boys. They use Tempests, Typhoons and Spits in defence. (Talking of fighters, 3 Gp was nibbled at the other day near Coblenz losing in the region of 20 Halibags. One day 5 Gp will run into a load of GAF and lose half the force.) This attack by Von Rundstedt has sort of shaken everyone round here. He's done darned well. When you have a look at the country he advanced over from the air you can see how he did it though. He seems to have had the met. taped too. They've had their time though, that's a cinch.

Old Bing has just sung 'Day after Tomorrow' and almost bust me in two.

Wednesday 3 January: Early this morning Nels. Hill and Dixie roll in well under way and begin a very good session of amusement by putting each other's pyjamas in the fire! Win is very niggly.

This evening I run Darkie and Geoff down to the dish and fip shop in Hykham village (I have had an offer of seven pounds for the car). Well now that all the celebrations of the end of 1944 have finished, I cannot help thinking back over the past year. The (main) thing I think about instantly is the LA and Pat. I wish she'd never joined the damned thing. She just loves the work of course, but does the work love her? There's going to be one big stink if I get back and she's changed at all. It appears as though I must see another winter through over here. I never want to go through a third at any cost. I'm just miserable, its so damp and cold. It's funny that I have never been in dock since joining up — another year, and still I've not been crook. How much more experienced I am now in almost every way. Before I finished a tour I know I didn't fear death. Now that I've finished I'm not too happy. It would be a shame to go for a burton now on a training flight. It's because I want to go home again so much I think.

Thursday 4 January: Dixie Hagley and I catch the 9 o'clock shuttle to Waddo after breakfast, where I get some money. We hitch hike to Lincoln and catch the 10.30 to London. I go to the Boomerang Club. At 1645 a V-2 rocket falls somewhere nearby and scares the daylights out of me. There are two more V-2 rockets during the evening and some during the night. Only a few V-1s came over within hearing of this locality. All day however V-2s have been arriving with characteristic unexpectedness. I can well understand people leaving London, although the chances of being killed are fairly remote. The bombs seem to land along a line roughly joining East Croydon and the Cockfosters-Hampstead Heath area, but there is a flat spot in its middle which luckily is London proper, where little or no bombs fall. They make an awful explosion leaving a deep crater, but have less blast effect than V-1, which is a good thing. Several fall during the night, one falling at Edgware, some 10 miles away.

Monday 8 January: Many V-2s fell yesterday.

This morning in London I order a new uniform from Carr Son and Woor. I buy myself a few oddments, and after lunch I go to see '30 secs. over Tokyo' — a damned good film, with Buff Hanna, whom I meet at the Boomerang Club. During the show, at 1630 a rocket falls quite close, shaking the whole theatre terribly.

Back at the Boomer I meet Brian Graves. He has just returned from Italy in a Stirling. We have tea together with Jack Yoeman (Western Junction type). Afterwards we go to the Savoy Tavern for a few drinks. During tea time a rocket falls, immediately followed by another one — shaky do.

Tuesday 9 January: I get up to find 6 inches of snow has fallen in the V-free night. It is very cold and still snowing at breakfast. I catch the 1105 from Paddington for Henley-in-Arden and after a cold uninteresting ride, changing at Leamington and Wilmcote, I reach Henley at about 1500. I go to the Blue Bell and check in. Then I walk down to 'Blackford' where the Sparks live. Mr Spark has invited me to fish in his strip of water — about 5 miles of the River Alne runs through his property. It holds trout up to about a pound and a half. This sounds wizard, I'll have to get Snake in on this show as he will be here longer than I and is sure to get on well with Sparkie if I introduce him.

Of the 12,000,000 odd homes in Britain 36,000 are over 280 years old and 4,500,000 are over 80 years old. This I found out today.

Thursday 11 January: This morning I write two Air Letters, one home and one to Pat. It snows all morning and it is very cold even indoors. I therefore take up my position right in front of the fire, sipping sundry IPAs. After dinner I set off to Oldburrow arriving there at about 3 pm. I meet Mrs Baldwin and tell her about Hank — all except that I know he's dead.

Friday 12 January: This morning the thaw sets in. I write to Pat beside the fire. In the afternoon I bus to the Olde Bull Inn, Wootton Wawen — my old haunt of just 12 months ago. A few drinks and then a meal (grilled ham, chips and green peas). Then lounge and sit beside the fire. (There are two new barmaids I see!)

Monday 15 January: While waiting for the 1152 bus to Birmingham a bloke pulls up in a Vauxhall 14 and takes me there in a couple of jiffs. I catch the 1320 to Derby and change to the Notts train, getting there at about 1500. I find I have to wait until 1723 for a Lincoln train, so I check my luggage in and go up to the Overseas Club for a snack (toasted buns, jam and tea). I meet a couple of Aussies here and natter a bit. One is a navigator from F/O Gibberd's crew. (61 SQDN.) Eventually I'm away and get to Hykham. En route I talk to a bloke just back from the Ardennes battle. He is very interesting. I am very sorry for our fellows over there — and the Jerries, if I could be. The cold must be awful. I walk to the Mess and lo! — a wizard heap of mail, including two wonderful letters from Pat. She's wizard, and I'm not kidding! I find that F/O Corewyn and his complete crew were killed on return from Museburg, near Leipzig. 50 have two missing from this trip. They have done Munich, again, also a place just north of Bordeaux and several bulge bashing shows (Sears went on one of these).

Gordie and Dixie have been posted to Warrington, to go home. Pop

Nugent is posted and the Adj. has gone overseas. I go down to the boy's hut. Bill has finished and is in Edinburgh. I believe he may even take the girl home — a wizard fellow Bill. I find Geoff just back. He has been recalled from leave and posted to Brackla. Darkie has already gone there. Geoff is to see the G/C and AOC before he goes. F/O Mouritz got shot up by an 88 off Denmark coming home from Polentz (synthetic oil plant near Stettin) — damned lucky to be alive, he may weave a little in future.

PART 5

RETURN TO AUSTRALIA

Tuesday 16 January 1945: I begin getting cleared. I am posted to 1660 HCU Swinderby — God what a relief, no Wimpies. The old car goes bang on and it only takes me a short time to get finished up. After dinner I take Geoff down to the Fox and Hounds for a drink or two on the last night together, and, for me the last night on 61 Squadron. I wish I could stay here. I have become so attached to the place, and so friendly with so many people. We have a good time and return early. I pack my gear and go to bed.

Wednesday 17 January: I get up early and to Waddo to get finally cleared and most important, some money. I am pounced upon by the Base Adj who tells me I have to report at Lulsgate Bottom this afternoon. I tell him about Swinderby and he is dumbfounded and has a regular session with 61 Adj by phone. Still I have to go to 3 FIS today. Back at 61 I find the mistake. I am to go to Swinderby after I finish this FIS Course.

I panic around and wangle a ride down in C-Charlie with F/O Boland. I say goodbye to those I can in the short time, sell the car to F/O Byers for six pounds and away we go. From Skelly to Coventry we go at about 50 ft — my gawd do I twitch. The first time in my life I think. We get to Lulsgate OK in 47 mins! Much better than 9 hours by train. The Lanc causes a stir and panic.

At once I find the place dispersed but likeable. I go to the mess from F/C per tranny. There are Oxfords, Harvards, Masters, Dakotas and Magisters here. The place is all up and down and I find my billet some 300 ft up above the airfield on a hillside. The mess is some 200 ft below the airfield! Although things are miles apart, once you get there they are wizard.

Saturday 20 January: I have settled in by now and know the ropes. I am here for 6 weeks approximately and there should be a little leave at the completion of the Course. This Course is not to teach you to fly, but to teach you how to teach others how to fly and they say that after 42 hrs here you can really fly yourself! It has been extraordinarily cold and there have been frequent snow and sleet showers. On Thursday there was a gale, which, in some parts of England reached 100 mph. This is the worst of its kind in history. I have begun flying the beaut Oxford. It's so long since I flew them I find them quite strange, but a piece of cake to handle. I have to get up 42 hours here. I went to Bristol one evening. I find it not much different to any other English town of any size that I have visited — no cleaner, no brighter and no less full of very nice people. It is some 7 miles from the camp here.

My word the Russians are doing well. They are 50 mls from Breslau and 190 mls from Berlin by tonight's news. C'mon Joe, give it to 'em and let's get home to the wife!

Tuesday 23 January: On waking up I find the place almost snowed under. This is the heaviest fall of snow I have ever seen. In some places it is piled about 4 feet high. Of course we don't fly today, instead we sit around doing SFA. I write to Pat. After lunch, however a magnificent snowfight develops in which the whole station from the CO, W/C Franklin DSO, DFC and bar, downwards is involved. I have become very friendly with a Leut O'Shea FAA who declares that he can get me home on a carrier, or at least a heavy cruiser. This would be wizard, so long as we didn't have any engagements en route! (In the snowfight I ripped, rather I split, my trousers from beam to beam amidships — frightfully embarrassing do!).

Berlin is 165 miles from the Red Army after their latest advances.

Wednesday 24 January: I receive the heavenly news that I am to be posted back to Australia, much to the envy and horror of other Australians here, especially Peter Ward. I am very happy about the whole affair of course. However I do feel I should like to have finished this course off. It would be definitely beneficial. I buy drinks all round.

Thursday 25 January: I sleep in this morning. It is terribly cold and snow has again fallen throughout the night. When I do get up about midday I am astonished to find the whole landscape quite covered in deep snow leaving only things higher than 3 to 4 feet protruding. I have never of course seen snow like this before. The taps are all frozen up. On arrival at the Mess I am told that the CO has decided to close the station up for 3 days as it is quite hopeless expecting any break for flying. I ring for a taxi and at 1500 Peter and I set off for London, where we manage to get in at the Howard Hotel — in the Bridal Suite!

Friday 26 January: Just as I get up there is an enormous explosion which rocks the building. They must be getting better sighting for V-2. About time. I see Carr Son and Woor and my uniform is ready — good show. Up at OHQ they tell me I should have posting instructions home by this time. It seems that a draft is expected to leave early in February and return hope via Suez. This is contrary to my expectations and hopes. However, if correct, it will complete a trip round the world for me.

Saturday 27 January: V-2 pounds down constantly shaking the daylights out of me.

I receive a wire from base requesting I return unit immediately. Evidently my posting is in. I panic around and catch the 4.15 from Paddington. A rocket falls very close as I enter the station and I can see the mushroom of smoke rising quickly up. The train is very late getting in at Bristol and to make matters worse I have to wait some time amongst a rowdy mob of Yanks for a taxi. On the way out my feet get so cold that they feel almost unbearably hot. I have heard people complain of cold feet before but this is the first time I can say I understand what it means. Maybe I'm getting old. I am really almost frozen when I reach camp. It costs me 12/-. I have a couple of beers in the Mess before going to bed, all by myself in a very cold hut with no fires. There have been no fires for two days either. I go to sleep with 3 jumpers on and all my clothes on top of the bed.

Sunday 28 January: It snowed again during the night. I get up and simply freeze. Boy!, will I be glad to get home to a little sunshine. Getting cleared is no joke and I smash two bikes in the process. (The sprocket gear freezes up and slips.)

At lunch I say goodbye to all I know including Wally and the Admiral. At 1500 transport takes me to Bristol. I check my case through to Brighton. At 1718 the train pulls out and I have a most tiring, dirty, cold and uneventful trip to London arriving at Paddington half an hour late. I get in at the Howard again and go straight to the Boomer then, to answer my own wire! Later we all go to Mick's for supper. I meet Jack Cottman PFF here. After the old steak and chips we go back to my pub for a while. It is late when the boys leave and I am not surprised when I hear they are back again to spend the night, their train long since having departed and the station locked and barred. We have a couple of drinks and then to bed. I have much to speak to Jack about, but I don't like to talk in front of Sue on these matters.

Monday 29 January: <u>MY BIRTHDAY</u>! Up we get and of course a rocket drops to wake me up completely. We have a late breakfast at the Boomer. Here I meet Tommy Noon from 97. He's done 23 now. I'm sure he'll get through too. Being my birthday today and Pat's on 4th February there is no better time for me to send her a cable announcing my return than now, so off Snake and I go. I have a quick lunch, arrange to meet Snake tomorrow, and am just on the way to catch a train to Lincoln when I run into Jock. I only have time for a few words and rush away to nail a taxi to Kings Cross where I only just manage to get on the train. A seat is quite out of the question so I stand in the corridor. Here begins a most cheesing and tiring trip, not to mention freezing. I stand as far as Peterborough where I manage to pounce on a seat. The train becomes increasingly late as we travel on, and in the compartment is a most repulsive and objectionable lady full of moans and stupid remarks. I try to sleep. Although this is a first class compartment it is about 10th class in cleanliness. I am not at all amazed to find that we have missed our connection at Grantham and so have to proceed via Sleaford. This journey in itself takes an hour and a half and it is no wonder I'm cheesed when I finally get to Lincoln.

I find all the taxis inoperative due to the heavy snow but after waiting 25 mins standing in slushy snow up to the ankles I get a bus as far as Doddington Road. The walk warms me up a bit but tires me out a lot and to make things worse it begins to snow half way. The meal in the mess is dreadful and the mess is almost deserted. Pexton is on leave and also Ernie Vale. The boys haven't operated since Brux so are a bit cheesed off.

Tuesday 30 January: I get up at 0800. At once things are grim because it has snowed again during the night. F/O Byers, now DFC, gives me three pounds at breakfast — good thing. At 0900 I am on the post office door and at 0915 it opens to let me get my great coat, which I put on at once. It is a wizard coat. All goes fine as far as Grantham, but here I find my connection will be at least one hour late. At length after a stinking trip I get to London (Kings Cross) at 4.45 instead of 2.5 pm. I go direct to the Boomerang Club and find Snake, have a snack, and go to the Howard where we have a clean up. I feel like nothing on earth, with a slight headache coming on. After tea we have a few drinks with Tom Noon at the Savoy Tavern before returning to the hotel. I don't feel too lively at all. Maybe it is because of all the travelling in the train or because I'm getting a cold, I don't know. I find it difficult to get to sleep.

Wednesday 31 January: We get up about 1000 and I don't feel much better. We go up to OHQ for some money, and, as Snake takes longer than me I go on to Carr Son and Woor for my new uniform. I call at Hardy Bros. on the way back to the Boomer. I have a little tea. I am not too bright still. Afterwards I meet F/O George, my old LFS instructor. He is going home also. Baz turns up and he and I decide to do a quiet pub crawl to spend the evening. We start at the Irish House and then go on to about 30 odd other pubs. We have quite a good time and at one stage of the game we are intercepted by a pair of crows (prostitutes) who are keen to play. We drop 'em pronto. We have supper at the Wentworth (or Imperial) and return to the hotel. Unsteadily I go to the cot.

Thursday 1 February: Lord, the second month in 1945 already. This morning I fill in oodles of forms and then finally am told I'm not wanted until Monday morning. I spend the afternoon poking around Brighton buying the odd thing here and there.

Friday 2 February: Up at 0900, have breakfast at the Canadian Legion and set off to London in the 1040. From Victoria we go straight to the Boomer and have lunch. Here I meet Bowland, Greenfield and Tom Noon. After lunch we go up to OHQ and do our business. I leave and return to Brighton. At the station here I enquire about my trunk and am sent off to the Metropole to find it. I find the place shut, so I go upstairs to see whether I'm the next draft. I am told I am not. On the way downstairs I run smack into Bill Jackman. I'm very pleased and surprised of course. Bill and I spend the afternoon and evening together having odd drinks at numerous pubs. At 2215 a large force of heavy bombers goes out across the coast in a south-easterly direction. We stand on the seafront and watch all the tiny lights until the last one disappears and the mighty roar dies away. We wish them luck aloud for we know too well what they'll meet and see. Some of those boys will die tonight, some will be wounded and some will bale out. I wish them all a good trip and wonder deeply where they are going.

Monday 5 February: This morning there is a heavy mist, almost a fog. I report at 0900 and find that I am neither on 70 nor 71 draft. I can't moan, because others have waited for longer than me. I'm a cert for the next. I see 'Slave Ship' and 'Wing and a Prayer' and then I am completely and absolutely flat broke, having placed my last half crown in the Red Cross box at interval! Tomorrow I must get some money.

Wednesday 7 February: Got home okay. Assuming the distance between launching site and place of strike of V-2 to be 200 miles. The maximum height to be 70 miles, the average speed 1000 miles/hour it would take the bomb 12 minutes in flight. However the sound would take 16 minutes. If one had good enough hearing therefore the noise of the bomb being launched, which is reputed to be audible within a radius of 7 miles anyway, could be heard 4 minutes after it landed. There is, after V-2 has exploded, an eerie rumbling like distant thunder. This, in my opinion, is the noise the bomb is making on its way down 1.3 miles up in the air. It lasts for some 30 seconds. On some occasions I have distinctly heard minor explosions amongst this rumbling. It is estimated thatV-2 weighs 13 tons at the time of launching and the initial reaction produces a resultant vertical force of twice its weight. The launching platform is almost on the horizontal and there is therefore no need for stabilisers or supports, the bomb stands upon its four fins. Reports indicate that before launching considerable stoking is necessary for some 30 minutes. When actual launching takes place personnel take cover in concrete pens if possible or other suitable places if launching is taking place on open ground. Actual launching is effected by means of electrical equipment some distance away. V-2 is transported to sites from dumps on 60 ft trailers. The destructive properties of V-2 are fortunately less than that of V-1. The blast effect is mostly shielded by the sides of the deep crater it makes deflecting the blast vertically. Of course any objects in the immediate vicinity are shattered. I hope the Hun is prevented from using improved V weapons if these two are what he calls prototypes. V-1 activity is now almost negligible. I am not wanted here until Monday next. There is considerable panic going on as the boys prepare for their voyage. 71 draft is leaving soon after 70. 72 will leave early in March I suppose. It will be good to get home but I can't say that I'm looking forward to the trip itself.

I believe there is an investiture at the Palace on the 13th of this month. Nels Hill will be on it, so will I for that matter. DFC each.

Thursday 8 February: It is announced that 15 persons were either killed or injured in a York which pranged into the sea on the way to the meeting of the Big 3 somewhere in the Black Sea area — darned good job that old Winston wasn't in it himself.

Tonight as I go up towards the clocktower I run into Dusty Millar from 61. He is staying with his wife down here. Of course I ask him the gen. Things are a bit grim it appears. 50 OTU have lost two. Old Lipton, an English second tour bod, has gone. 6 are safe, but they don't know which 6. S/L Hugh Horsely lost an engine — the port outer on T/O. He tried to do a circuit as best he could. The bomb load was a 'cookie' and clusters, and he almost made it onto the 25 runway but couldn't and landed just off it. The 4000 pounder and clusters went up. Nothing remained of 6 of the crew, but extraordinarily enough the rear gunner was blown clear. Hugh was a good type, and I'm sorry to hear this news. He was shot down over Holland before, but evaded to rejoin the Squadron. I wonder what I would have done in the same position. I think I would have tried to make the sea and jettison. The explosion shook everything and broke windows in Lincoln 5 miles away.

Sunday 11 February: Alf Copley has arrived to return home so I have a friend now with whom to spend the much spare time I have on hand. He tells me that Bill Watson is permanently grounded as a result of his collapse on a trip. Old 'Lime' and Arthur Plowman have gone for a burton. A most enormous box of dried fruits and nuts arrives from Pat. I have never in all my life seen a box its size. It appears I am unable to let ᴀᵉr know it has arrived either, for security reasons. Never mind I'll tell her myself shortly!

During January V-bombs killed 585 and injured 1,629. This is the highest death toll since last August when 1,103 were killed, and 2,921 were injured. The peak month was July — 2,441 killed and 7,107 injured.

Tuesday 13 February: Alf and I go to London on the 1108 and eventually get in at the Grand Hotel in Southampton Road. It is always difficult to get in on a Tuesday in London. We get a double room for 33/- per night. We meet Des, Kell and Nels at the Strand Palace where, in the Grill Room, we have lunch. Afterwards we go to see Greer Garson and Walter Pidgeon in 'Mrs Parkington' at the Palladium. I find it a characteristically wonderful film for these two, and thoroughly enjoy every minute of it. We have dinner at the Salted Almond and then go on the Codger's, Mick's and to our respective Hotels. As yet I have heard no V-2s.

Wednesday 14 February: We get up at 0930, bath, and then Alf and I part. He sets off for Manchester and I go down to the Strand Palace to find the boys just getting up. I am both sad and amazed to learn that F/O Collins, RAAF, F/O Tasker, RAF and F/Lt Bartlett RAF are missing from this latest raid on the synthetic oil plants at Politz. Coll was a champion fellow and he had a wizard crew. Bartlett, I am particularly sorry to hear such news about. He had a most lovely wife whom he brought back from Canada. They had a wizard little son too.

We have lunch at the Boomerang Club. I have a haircut downstairs. Afterwards Des and I go and get some seats for 'Is your Honeymoon really necessary?' at the Duke of Yorks Theatre. Coming back I collect my 8 ft Casting Club de France rod from Hardy Bros in Pall Mall. I manage to get an aluminium case for it also which is very satisfactory.

Later when we are all in the Strand in Nels' room a shattering explosion announces a rocket. It lands somewhere up towards Aldwich, Kingsway from what we can understand. We go for a walk in this direction to see if we can find where it lands. This is in vain however and after a couple of drinks in a tiny pub we go on to the show. On the way back again, just as we are coming down Pall Mall towards Trafalgar Square there is a vivid flash ahead followed some four seconds later by the most terrible explosion. Just as we are getting over this another one lands not far away. We estimate that they are some 4/5ths of a mile away from us. In a matter of moments we hear the sirens of the ambulances and ARP wagons.

Thursday 15 February: Down near Trafalgar Square a sinister looking figure appears and questions us about the possibility of some nearby A/R shelters being open. Being a sucker I take a look, in order to help, and find that everything is well locked up. This is a very poor show for our friend, for he has no bed and claims he spent every night last May in these shelters. He presently begins rambling on about the water in the ponds, the possibility of rockets falling and the nature of the weather, and I believe, one or two other things. Just as I am about to announce that we two are becoming cheesed and are therefore leaving he comes closer, and then to my half-amazement and my friend's horror he draws a long bladed knife from his left hand pocket. Before he has time to use it, if he was going to use it, I slide him on his ear, the knife going one way, his dark hat another and his walking stick another, he himself uttering a deep grunt like a contented pig. I have no idea which one of us he intended doing, or whether it was both, far less can I think of a motive — money being right out of the question. We make our way most expeditiously to the tube station without further incident.

Friday 16 February: Des has a terrible head this morning. I say cheerio to Nels and Kell and then at Kings Cross station I say the same to Des before catching the Lincoln train. En route to the station I see where a V-2 landed yesterday. There is a most extraordinary mess, and an enormous hole. Three or four large buildings have been severely damaged. Digging in the debris is still in progress. I have to stand to Peterborough but from then on I get a seat. I catch a bus to the station and am just in time for tea. I meet all the boys of course — those that are left, and get the gen on Horsley's prang. Pexton to my disappointment, has been posted to 21 Group TC. Crampton is back again.

Sunday 18 February: This morning I go and have a look where Horsley blew up. There isn't a piece of aeroplane larger than 2' x 4' left to be found (except I believe the engines and main spar which have been taken away). The crew in P at the time (Cunsworth) and the ground boys were awfully lucky not to go up too, especially Bill and Mac who ran towards the runway when they saw it coming only to find it 'following them'.

Tonight I go to the Plough with the boys from the kite and Jimmy Meus too. We have a very decent evening. It has been wizard to come back here again and see all the blokes again, and well worth the long train ride. I see old Ward, my appo at Lulsgate Bottom and also Jimmy Davies have got their gongs. Also old Frogley!

Monday 19 February: Up early for breakfast and I say cheerio to all the chaps I know, including the G/C and S/L Fadden. I meet Jock at Lincoln and astonishingly enough we get a seat all the way and a room in the Howard. We have a snack at the Boomer, go to 'Woman in the Window', have another snack and then proceed on a crawl finishing up at Mick's cafe. Jock runs away with a couple of girls most expeditiously.

I have to decide whether to stay in England until after DFC investiture by the King at Buckingham Palace or get on the next available draft back home to Pat.

Thursday 22 February: Begin getting cleared. I receive a letter from W/C Pexton ('Dick!'), also Jock and Joan. I have decided to buy a sports coat. Tonight Alf, myself and our old A/G friend go to see Max Miller at the Hippodrome. He's a very crude type of comedian, but he pleases these people — they are certainly crude, and a lot of them just down-right disgusting.

Tonight whilst in the Arlington for supper I see 3 Yanks and 3 English girls having a snack. The girls are about 18 odd and are trying to eat — the American way — with the fork only! Alf and I are outwardly amused and almost cause a brawl.

Wednesday 28 February: Well it's all organised now. I am on No. 77 Draft. It appears that we are leaving here on Saturday night some time. This is not definite yet as I have heard a rumour that the date has been postponed to the 8th. I have bought a great deal of stuff to take home, especially for Pat. I have also got hold of a lot of cigarettes. I only hope the Customs people don't get any silly ideas or that the trunk doesn't become mislaid en route. I am not at all looking forward to this boat trip. Once that ship begins climbing and diving I begin to withdraw into my shell for the entire journey. I think I shall try smoking cigars this time to fill in time and amuse and content myself.

Monday 5 March: I am astounded and amazed to be able to vouch for any statement regarding the fine work done by RAF intelligence people. When I visited Shellingthorpe not long ago I heard much talk about the possibility of intruders and scalded cat raiders making a reappearance at any time. Elaborate precautions and even preparations were being made against such attack much to the amusement and scorn of all the boys. Of course, why not, I should have felt the same, the idea would have seemed fantastic to me during my latter operations. I used to turn my nav. lights on when crossing the English coast — why the blackout restrictions in Lincoln were even partly lifted, in fact all round this area. Yet there it was, early on the morning of March 3rd, and yesterday morning again there was considerable enemy activity over N and Southern England. Many small bombs were dropped and a number of incendiaries and there were a number of machine-gunning incidents reported. Naturally there were casualties and damage.

On the first night 6 A/C were shot down over Britain and 2 at their home airfields. And the most interesting point about it is that Waddington and Skellingthorpe were attacked by an 88. Two Halifaxes were shot down nearby by a 410. Several men were killed at the Waddington bomb dump where some incendiaries were alight. I have had no first-hand information regarding damage or casualties at Skellingthorpe. Nor have I had any reliable information about yesterday morning's show, apart from the fact that it was on a smaller scale. The Hun. A/C engaged were 88s, 188s, 410s, 109s and 190s. There is a possibility that jet 262s and 163s were also in use but there has been no confirmation.

V-1 — Doodlebug activity has also been resumed in some strength, launched, it is believed from ramps built behind the front. The fly bombs appear to be larger and have longer range. Therefore London has had a touch of both V-1 and 2 for the last couple of days. On the other hand, the new offensive on the Western Front is going well and Cologne and Duisburg appear doomed. The whole Rhur valley will fall unless the Hun does something brilliant in a hurry.

77 and 78 drafts have been combined and we are now all 78. The date still stands as the 8th. I hope it is not scrubbed again. It is a bind that I cannot communicate with anyone but still to safeguard my own neck and that of many other blokes it is wise to be quiet. I have met a very interesting type by the name of Paul Palfery 424920.

Tuesday 6 March: Tonight a big force of Lancs passes out across Beachy Head heading towards France. I wonder where they are heading for tonight. It gives you quite a thrill to see them all going out across the coast in a great procession. So many times I have looked down upon Beachy Head myself as we were going out, and I always used to get a lump in my throat.

Thursday 8 March: Last night we decided to celebrate our last evening in England and this we did in no mean fashion, shaking Brighton town considerably. But it was a lot of fun. The boys went to Dessau, SW of Berlin the other night — 30 missing. PM Paul, Alf, Geoff and myself go to a show in Hove and, after tea, to another before catching our bus to the station. Now this being an occasion of note, many of the boys have been soaking 'em down, with the result that I have never in all my life seen such a scene of utter bedlam on the station platform. The noise and bustle having aroused both the curiosity and amusement of the natives. I am not surprised to find a large civilian crowd forming. Paul and I manage to get in with a moderately sober crowd and settle down. Already my fly-rod, which I have been obliged to carry due to its awkward length, has caused some amusement amongst the less trout-minded members of the draft. At length, then after what seems an age of waiting, we draw out of the station at 2307 and I learn from OC Draft that we stop at Sheffield at 0620 for 20 minutes and we are due at Liverpool at 0945. I am thankful we are to leave from here and not Glasgow, Grenock or some other far northern port.

It strikes me as being queer, but neither Paul nor myself are the slightest bit worried about this whole business. We only caught the bus by 7 minutes. I suppose it is because we have become used to the idea of moving about, having done so much of it, and this trip although leading us home, and to all that means, over some thousands of miles of ocean, is no different to any other shift we've made.

And so after a little while we both drop off to sleep, and I myself sleep off and on until Sheffield where we bounce out for a cup of hot tea. It is bitterly cold so we bounce inside again, and are soon under way once more. I sleep until dawn and then have a last look about the English countryside before we pull into a siding at Aintree just out a bit from Liverpool city. Here we get aboard buses and proceed thus to the docks. Of course everyone is wondering the same thing — what sort of tub is it? At length we get out of the buses and catch our first glimpse of her — a medium sized affair of some 20,000 tons. It is not until some time later after I have been aboard for awhile that I discover that the name is the 'Empress of Scotland' — used to be the 'Empress of Japan', a Canadian Pacific ship. I have a cabin with 3 others, with all mod cons, and I expect I shall be quite happy.

During the afternoon, after an extremely good lunch which I was in need of very much, Paul and I spend the time wandering around the ship making ourselves familiar with all the gangways, decks, alleyways, stairs etc. and by tea time we are again in need of a good meal. So when they serve out steak, we are all for it in a big way. Afterwards at 1930 we have boat drill and become familiar with our various muster stations and how to get to them.

Having not been to bed for 48 hours I decide that it's not a bad place to be in, and so get in, finding little trouble in getting to sleep.

Saturday 10 March: Paul almost dies of shock when I wake him at 0700 this morning. We go to breakfast at 0730 after reading the Daily Express, which is lowered to us on the hook of one of the dock cranes by a sympathetic crane operator. On coming from breakfast we find much activity afoot for we are casting off. At 0800 exactly we begin to move away from our docking, and for the next two hours we are pushed, pulled, twisted and turned by tugs as we move out through the maze of docks and piers into the river itself and finally to the channel proper where we make our way between a series of buoys, where at the last pair we stop to let the pilot off. Just before lunch we pick up several more quite large troop ships and two destroyers. It appears therefore that we are to proceed in convoy. It is a cold cloudy day and I get my last glimpse of England through a mist-like smoke haze. After lunch we are 6 ships strong, plus the two warships, and at 1315 we see land which we believe is either the Isle of Man or somewhere around the Solway Firth. Evidently we are to pick up more ships en route from the Clyde and Solway before nipping off round the North tip of Ireland and down south. First stop I believe is Gibraltar.

When first I learnt that I was to come to England I was very thrilled. This was quite natural I am sure and I was no different to any other fellow. I had read so much and been told so much about England ever since I could remember — its history from the earliest days right up to the present time, and last of all the war that I believed had hit her so hard. I believed that London was battered almost to ruins and also Coventry, Birmingham, Bristol, Hull, Portsmouth and the rest. I believed that the people were starved and without clothing. I believed in short that England was a battle-scared island of heroes. And when I came I found how incorrect my idea and opinion of England was, and now, after living in and seeing most of it for 18 months I have learnt that what I found in those first few days at Brighton stands good for all war-time England, and, to a certain extent Scotland.

I found London still standing, with here and there a building knocked out and the same state of affairs at the other blitzed cities. I found the people had plenty to eat and not much worse off than the people I left at home, certainly you could buy much more stuff than, at home, I know was almost impossible. Bike tyres and tubes, light bulbs, torches, soap, tooth brushes, cigarettes and a host of other things were almost over plentiful. Clothes were hard to get at home not only because of coupons, but also because in many cases the article was not to be had anyway. I found the clothing shops with their windows crammed full of things over here. There were of course some things, and there still are, in very short supply such as eggs, sugar, fountain pens and good pipes.

Sunday 11 March: I get up to find we have quite a roll on. It is a cloudy, cold, misty morning but after breakfast it clears a little and the sun rises through a breaking in the strato cumulus cloud. By it we make our course roughly West. Later on in the morning we join up with some more ships and an escort carrier. Altogether we are 15 ships strong now plus an escort of 5 destroyers and the carrier. The sea becomes quite choppy after lunch and several WRENS go for the big spit! However I have not yet made a glorious rush for the taffrail or bucket or any other receptacle. Feel very fit indeed due, I have no doubt, to the exercise Paul and I enjoy by walking up and down the quarter deck 120 times to one mile.

I can see, however, that I am going to become very bored indeed with four weeks of this business. Never shall I want to see water in such abundance again in my life. Paul and I have found for ourselves a small but adequate window on the starboard quarter of the ship on A deck where we spend a lot of time looking out. We are on this side of the convoy it so happens, and subsequently all we can see is water and two of our destroyer escort, one near and one far out. On the other side of the ship there is the convoy to be seen and the presence of these other ships does lend a little interest to the otherwise boring sight of an endless expanse of sea as far as the eye can see. Towards evening we become increasingly enveloped in mist and one by one the other ships become invisible, until none at all can be seen. At this stage a queer affair is let out and trailed behind which produces a fountain of foaming water. On sight of this any ship overtaking us at once knows of our position and takes the necessary avoiding action. Today we were close enough to the carrier to recognise the A/C on her flight deck as Seafires. I am hoping that they will do a little flying over there some time.

As was the custom on other troop ships I have been on, we carry at all times our life preservers. Never are you allowed to be without it. It is even present when having a bath, at meals and when visiting the little place. On this ship we have also been issued with a small floating torch and a tin of emergency rations which we must also carry at all times. The temptation to open any issue of this nature immediately is very great, but OC troops forewarns us regarding this lot. We have to hand them in again at the end of our journey or pay for them and apart from this, his dog had rejected the contents once he declares so it can't be anything too tasty inside.

A study of my map of Southern England tells me that if I take a line from Reading to Portland Bill, the route we so frequently took both leaving and returning to England, the line passes almost directly over Stockbridge on the Test. I often looked down at and along the river and sometimes flew low but we were always tired coming home and keen to get there. So I know the Test well. We sometimes did a circle or two around Windsor Castle which is just a little off track, to see who was there and check the place out. And Chilbolton too where Jack Clark lives and I have an open invitation to fish.

Tuesday 13 March: There is a fiery red sunrise this morning and so I predict poor weather later on today. The rumour has spread about that today some time we are to leave the convoy and proceed on our own to and through the Panama canal. Now this is indeed a poor show in my opinion if it turns out to be true. I very much would prefer to go through the Mediterranean and thereby complete a voyage round the world. Paul is of the same opinion and we set about putting down such a rumour for it makes us mad, mainly because we have a funny feeling it is going to be true.

During the afternoon the escort vessels indulge in a little practice and drop depth charges, fire guns and fire up a magnificent AA barrage including rockets to conclude with. Lo and behold at 1815 we alter course, increase speed and leave the convoy. This is indeed a blow. Panama it is most certainly, and so, no round the world cruise. This is a trifle now as a new and yet more severe blow has hit me. We shall be disembarked at Sydney and not Melbourne. I am not, even at this early stage, looking forward to the train trip between. I believe it takes 16 days to go from Panama to Sydney. I'll go nuts, that's all about it.

After tea Paul and I look out through our little hole and all there is to be seen is water. On the other side is water. There are no ships now; not a sausage! The clocks go back 1 hour at midnight so I'll get another hour of sleep — this is some, but little consolation.

Friday 16 March: As in 'The Ancient Mariner' it's water water everywhere and pretty boring, so I'll take the opportunity to talk about operations more fully.

First, I must record my tremendous admiration and praise for the two WAAFs who controlled our landing procedure with such calm skill. To muster 40 Lancasters and get them airborne in 40 minutes was a credible achievement by the Ops Wagon crew, where crowds of off-duty personnel gathered to give each A/C the thumbs up. But to get them all down again in 40 minutes — probably tired, at night and maybe shot up was something quite different. Each girl handled one squadron, both 61 and 50 answering simultaneously. No emergency would flap them. They were marvellous and deserve special mention. If too many A/C came together they would stack us up one above the other or, in bad weather, vector us away on a timed return.

O B O E was the code name of a radar navigational aid which enabled PFF to mark certain targets in duff weather with accuracy. The system depended on the re-radiation from the A/C of radar signals sent to it. There are two ground stations. One controls the A/C, keeping it on a given course which passes directly over the target. The other measures how far it has gone along this course. When it is in the exact position when the TI's, or bombs, should be dropped a signal is sent. The system was, of course, improved from time to time and Mosquitos used it frequently.

H 2 S as an entirely different device from O B O E. This was contained wholly within the A/C and required no transmission from ground stations. Thus it could be used by any number of A/C at the same time. Objects on the ground, large buildings, coast lines, estuaries and built up areas could be detected through unbroken cloud or total darkness so that the navigator was able to mapread in any weather or conditions of light. The H2S marking technique was continuously improved especially by 5 group Pathfinders. The most successful H 2 S attack was carried out on the night of July 24–25. The target was Hamburg. Some 700 A/C attacked and the weather was favourable. Hamburg was particularly easy to identify by H 2 S. The attack caused gigantic fires which could not be put out even after 24 hours.

W I N D O W was the code name used for the strips of metallised paper (one strip about ½ inch for use against flak and the other about 2 inches wide against night fighters). We used to throw Window out of the A/C over enemy territory. When several hundred of us were doing this at the same time the result was the most effective defence against enemy radar.

I F F Identification Friend or Foe is installed in all operational A/C and consists of a pulse transmitter and receiver. Each day the code being transmitted, say A K, is changed so that any A/C not transmitting this signal must be hostile — a simple but most effective device that saved hundreds of A/C and lives, particularly whenever Jerry sent over sneak night fighters to join the circuit or just cruise on a seek and destroy mission.

D R E M This was the name of the special landing system which was installed at operational stations within Bomber Command and enabled four A/C to be controlled in the circuit at any one time, each of them able to hear the controller or each other, but no other A/C outside the circuit — one ingenious system.

G E E Des, my navigator, used this apparatus consistently. Two stations, a master and a satellite, simultaneously transmitted a pulse. Gee in the A/C measured the difference between the times that the two pulses were received, giving the distance the A/C was from each station. At the same time a second satellite station transmitted a pulse with the master station. By means of the Gee apparatus the navigator was then able to pinpoint the A/Cs position at the point of intersection of the two lines marked on the chart designed for Gee use.

P L U T O After D-Day a large pipe was laid under the Channel to the Cherbourg peninsula to carry petrol — Pipe Line Under The Ocean.

F I D O This was the name given to all airfields equipped with fog dispersal oil pipe lines down both sides of the runway which, when alight, generated heat which raised the cloud base. I landed at Fiskaton once where they had this system.

Bomber Command consisted of six Groups — Nos 1 and 3 Lancasters, 4 and 6 Halifaxes and 5 a special duty Group of Lancasters used for special operations such as the Dam Busters raid, the Tirpitz, U-Boat shelters etc. 5 Group virtually ended up as a separate identity with it's own P F F, night fighters and method of operation. It was the only Group to use the 12,000 lb Tallboy armour-piercing bomb and the 22,000 lb bomb Grand Slam. 11 Group Spitfires were used as a daylight escort.

Wednesday 21 March: The last few days have certainly warmed the cockels of my heart. We have all been attired in shorts and shirts, and for a while revelling in the joy of seeing and feeling the real sun again after so long a time. I have paid dearly for grabbing at too much sun for I'm almost frizzled up and a fiery colour. I have learnt that skin even accustomed to sunshine cannot, especially after some time without sun at all, stand up to too long in the sun of this Caribbean Sea. No wonder the pirates I read about who roamed these seas were inevitably bronzed. Today has been the hottest of all — a fair sizzler. I have carefully dodged the sun all day until sunset when all the kick had gone out of it. Then I sat on the sun deck in the cool and almost laughed at its last vain fiery red attempts to bake me redder than a lobster.

The numbers of flying fish have increased to flocks numbering perhaps 50 or 60. The seaweed I am informed is Caribbean Sea, Gulf stream weed. Below deck at night is like a furnace and I sleep, or try to in my birthday suit. The sweat trickles away all night until in the morning the bunk is quite wet. We are on A deck — I hate to think what it would be like on D deck! It is more a coma than a sleep that you fall into. Tomorrow we are due to dock at Christobel — Panama, early I believe. I am looking forward to seeing and maybe feeling dry land again very much. Yesterday we passed several islands at a distance and they were a wonderful sight. I'm sick and tired of this sea business. I am also looking forward to seeing just how the canal works. I have read about it and seen several photographs. However there is nothing like seeing a thing to reap the fullest benefit.

Thursday 22 March: Last night was terribly hot and I get up at 6 am this morning to get out for some fresh air and enjoy the cool breeze before the sun rises. At 0700 I see the first piece of land above the horizon. It is a great thing to see. Then several ships appear and smaller US Navy craft come out to meet us. Overhead one or two PBM-1s circle about. After breakfast we are much closer to shore and I can see the housetops shining white in the morning sun. This is Christobel and from out here some 4 miles away it looks wizard. Increasing numbers of aircraft appear. P 40s, P 38s and 39s, AT 11s and Mariners. We pick up a pilot and enter through a gap in the stone breakwater into a tidy little harbour with some 8 or 10 wharves. Some messing about goes on, but by 0930 we are safe and sound docked and tied up at No. 8 Wharf (built 1913). Everywhere there are coloured men. About one out of ten is white. It becomes quite hot when the sun gets up and Paul and I lean over the rail in the shade watching the niggers on the wharf fighting and squabbling over pennies that the boys toss down. When a brawl begins the boys cheer them on to good effect — well worth the pennies.

Round about there are odd patches of grass and numerous palm trees. All the houses have very flat gables and long shady eaves looking as cool as refrigerators. I should very much like to spend some time here looking around but at once I am decided that I shouldn't care very much to live here. The ship's surgeon, Commander Prendegast, tells Paul and I that he will be going ashore later and suggests that we accompany him as orderlies. Of course we are very enthusiastic about it and go off to dinner in great spirits. He says he will call us by tannoy when he is ready. After dinner we race about getting suitable clothes ready and on, waiting for the tannoy message. At about 1.45 it is announced that 1st Class passengers may proceed ashore independently. We wait for the message until about 2.15 when we become fed up and go to the Doc's office-come-cabin to find that he has disappeared. The steward comes and tells us he's gone ashore!

We go ashore for a wander about on the wharf. This is about as far as we manage to get for nobody is permitted out the gate into the town proper. However, being in a mood for murder we take delight in sneaking past NPs, MPs, SPs, CPs and any sort of Ps to see what we can. The town appears very interesting, with several large blocks forming the shopping and business centre. Tall palms line the streets where brightly polished modern cars are parked. There is a distinct line between the white and black living quarters, the former being some little distance removed from the town along the inland shore. Actually the place is about 30 times as long as it is wide, stretching along the waterfront, against a dense green jungle and steep, volcanic-looking little mountains. It is a very lively little place, the pubs being open until well after midnight and there are countless nightclubs, some obviously something else besides. One or two even have written signs to this effect. I believe the shows that are put on here are extremely hot.

This is what is called the dry season here. From May to December is the wet season when torrential rains are experienced almost daily, and when the humidity is something awful. The local inhabitants are dressed very lightly of course, but I note that shorts are not worn at all! Our shorts therefore are quite a source of amusement. All the white men seem to have a Panama hat which of course is quite appropriate.

Friday 23 March: I wake at 0600 odd and get up at about 0700 to find, by looking out through a port that we are away, moving slowly up a narrow waterway quite like any river, except that the vegetation on the banks is somewhat different. In place of grass, familiar trees, bushes and shrubs there is one great green mask. On looking closer it could be separated into broad-leafed ferns, creepers of many kinds, long bamboo-like grasses, palms and numerous mysterious and strange trees — the whole thing far too amazing for one to see first thing in the morning. So I pull my head in, and prepare for breakfast.

Afterwards Paul and I go out onto the sundeck, find a good elevated place to sit, and still very much amazed by the scenery already viewed, begin to be still further amazed. We have begun to pass through the canal. Soon we reach the first series of locks, 3 in all, named Gaton Locks taken from the lake farther up, and all of which serve to lift the ship up to the level of the lake. Here are another series of locks on the port side, so that two ships might pass through at the same time. This holds good almost all the way through the canal, but there are some places where one ship of any size scarcely has room, let alone two. We glide into the lock, stop, large gates close behind us — in comes the water and up we go, open the gates at the other end and on to the next — ditto repeato. We are towed along by electrically driven caterpillar tractors using the elastic steel cable idea. The whole procedure is intensely interesting although slow. On through the three lifting locks and we pass, with much whistle-blowing, into the fresh-water lake — Lake Gaton. It is announced that fresh water baths will be available now for at least 3 hours. On again through a maze of small islands overladen and top-heavy looking with jungle greenery. The only thing missing is the screech of parrots and monkeys! On all sides round the lake is bounded by volcanic hills. Overhead dark eagles circle. Paul and I decide to look for alligators. Slowly the channel we are following narrows down and the banks steepen and become more rugged. There are patches of light and dark brown amongst the green. Banana trees can be seen here and there, some laden down with enormous orange-yellow fruit. Very little wind reaches down into our valley and it is burning hot even in the shade, and although you don't look towards the sun the glare is intense. Lunchtime comes before we know it so we slip down to gobble our meal so as not to miss too much.

When we again look out there is scarcely 10 yards between the sides of the good ship only great jagged faces of rock may be seen. At length we pass a small village to port with hardly a white man to be seen. Numbers of black children leap about in excitement pointing and shouting. Old blackmen lean in the shade in huge straw hats, gay shirts and blue cotton pants. These are the true Panamanians. Very soon we pass another village similar to the first. On to the next lock. We are surprised to find ourselves let down instead of up. Out we sail into a small lake. Children paddle out in canoes, from scanty wooden huts on the bank where the live, scarcely larger than a garage. On again and a larger more modern town appears to post the roofs all painted dull red and some three storied buildings are present. Modern cars whiz about and a train pulls in at the station. Like Christobel, the streets here are lined with large palms. At the other end of the lake we enter another series of two locks, again letting us down. Like the others these too are double locks so that two ships may pass, or go together, and like the others they are guarded by many US Army guards. Round about are many AA guns and searchlights. These are the last locks. On we go through a larger waterway, the town giving place to large military stores, transport parks and great forests of radio masts. White herons fish along the banks and rise as we come near. One hits a wire as it climbs away and drops into the very long grass that now lines the banks. Little groups of people fish off odd small jetties on either side. And so we glide down to Gamboa, the town which marks the Pacific side of the canal. This really looks like a place where I could have a fine time. It is bright and colourful, with an abundance of shops, more trees, more people and in general more of it. Like all the other places, a little grey wooden church stands upon a mound shaded by palms and sprawling green trees with large leaves on all sides. I want very much to stop, even to stop the ship to look a little longer but on past it we go to the dock area. The first ship we pass, a freighter has a huge shell hole torn in the funnel — not very nice for us on our way out, to see. Here is real colour, paint of all colours catches the eye. There are canoes, motor launches, barges, ferries, ships of all sorts and size, birds and aeroplanes — red, green, brown, grey, yellow, white, blue, black — all colours, and we both remark upon it at the same time. Behind the dock there is an airfield and we glimpse aircraft from time to time standing in the sun. On each side now are great pieces of rock with fortifications and harbour-control buildings built on them. We can see the Pacific ahead. Through the anti-submarine boom with much whistling and we begin to pass between the strings of buoys lining the channel. Gamboa can be seen much better from out here a little, and it looks more attractive than ever. At the end of the channel we drop our pilot, in American Army uniform and glide on out to sea between a handful of islands over a dead calm sea as the sun begins to settle. Dirty grey pelicans swim and fly nearby, and one or two peculiar black birds with white necks pass overhead, with thin pointed wings and tail, and a tiny head. They appear to have a span of some 3 feet and are very fast, and nimble on the wing. Snakey-looking things, as Paul describes them.

Fifteen airacobras fly in from out to sea as the power is put on, and we begin the long journey towards home which, I understand, will take us 16 days. It has taken us about 10 hours to go from the dock in Christobel to the pilot barge out from Gamboa. We were in the actual canal zone for some 8½ hours. It has been a most interesting day there is no doubt, and an experience that I shall for ever remember. As the sun sets we are well into the Pacific, passing a few small islands to starboard then when they sink behind the horizon, nothing. You can smell the saltiness of the Pacific in the air, quite strongly at times. This is a characteristic not found with the Atlantic.

Sunday 25 March: Last night we crossed the equator — or maybe it was early this morning. Unfortunately the Master will not allow any form of ceremony of the Ancient Rights of the Deep to be conducted. In peacetime of course some big shows were often put on when the ship would slow down for King Neptune and his band of men to come aboard. All those who had not passed this way before were charged with humorous crimes and invariably found guilty when they would be ducked ceremoniously in a tub and well and truly soaked. And such was the case on the 'Mount Vernon' for all 1st Class passengers. But that was an American ship of course. However I believe some sort of certificate is being prepared for us all to mark the crossing. I have one already from my first crossing of the line.

Was it ever hot trying to sleep last night? I woke up this morning feeling like a washed out rag. Tonight the Southern Cross is just visible and I can't help feeling a sort of thrill at the sight of it. It will be so wizard to get back home to Australia. Talking of Australia, I don't think there's another country in the world as pure as we are. Pure I mean in blood. England and America are made up of all sorts of people from all parts of the globe. Especially now, England is a great jumble of different blooded people speaking different languages. And my not very large admiration for any of these mass-educated, animal-like repulsive 'pongoes' we have on board doesn't help me any too well when I think about them all being disembarked at Sydney and then sent to their different stations. Some time or other they'll have leave, and I can't but feel that somehow their very presence, let alone actions, will stain this land I like so much. For myself, and I am not alone in this thought, I should rather have the Americans about the place. After all I have seen a good bit of each country, town and field, and seen the people in the homes and watched the way they live, comparing it with our own way at home. I wouldn't give tuppence for the lot of them. People say the Americans are an immoral and sexual crowd when abroad and to a degree at home. I have seen all this. And I have also seen the disgusting way of things in England. The Yanks have a great deal to learn in this respect.

Friday 30 March: At length the hot weather seems to have broken. Today there is a cold wind blowing and quite a roll on. The Allied Armies are believed to be 200 miles inside Germany, and less than 200 miles from Berlin. Things are very much confused and no accurate pinpoint news seems to be available yet. This looks like the last phase of that part of the war. The next thing is to finish the Nips. I don't for one minute suspect it should, but it would be a dead loss if Jerry packed up while we were still at sea — a fine celebration we could have, I must say!

Tuesday 3 April: Just two years since I finished up at Deniliquin. The time has passed quickly. How much more experienced I am now to the way I was at Deni. This war business has had its advantages for me. I believe we are to cross the International Date Line on Wednesday. Therefore we'll get into Sydney on Sunday night or Monday morning. Lord knows what happens then. One thing is certain I'll not be doing any rushing hither and thither. It will be all just quiet, slow and steady progress.

Friday 6 April: Last night we crossed the International Date Line. Today should have been Thursday but it isn't, and as far as we are concerned never will be. Somehow or other we have caught up with it, flung ourselves at it, knocked it down and winded it and now shot past it never to see it again. Latest rumours suggest that we are due on Monday morning. Whether we are to disembark on Monday too or not I don't know. I certainly hope so.

I am becoming very restless. Today I put on my battle dress to begin with. After breakfast I go up on the sundeck in the sun. It's too hot up there so I come down and change into shorts and up again. This time it's too cold so I go to the lounge. It's still too cold there, so I go down to the cabin again and get my battle dress jacket and return to the lounge. Then I can't find anything to do. I smoke, drink lemonade and try to sleep. Finally I get a brainwave. I'll write a story about trout fishing. This has proved very successful so far for I have been at it continuously not even noticing the time slip by. People think I'm mad. I wonder who'll go mad first — me with writing or them with boredom?

Tuesday 10 April: What a magnificent day it is today. If it was teeming with rain it still would be. I have not had time to write these last few days for I have been too excited I think and therefore too restless. I'm home and still alive!

TERMS AND ABBREVIATIONS

A/C – Aircraft

a/c – Alter Course

A/G – Airgunner

A/H – Aft Hydraulics

A/I – Airborne interception

A/M – Abort Mission

A/P – Aiming point

A/W – All-up weight

ACK-ACK – Anti-aircraft gunfire

AFU – Advanced Flying Unit

AGONY MERCHANT – Dentist

AIRGRAPH – Reduced photo-reproduction of a letter

ALDIS LAMP – Hand-held electric signalling torch

ANGELS – Height

AOC – Air Officer Commanding

ARRIVAL – Poor landing

ARSE-UP – Upside down

ASI – Air Speed indicator

ATC – Air Training Corps

ATS – Auxilliary Transport Service

AXE – Killed

B/A – Bomb-aimer

B/H – Bombing height

B/S – Bomb sight

BAIL OUT – Parachute jump

BANDIT – Enemy aircraft

BANG ON – Good

BAT – Beam approach training

BEAM – Radio landing aid

BELLY LANDING – Landing without undercarriage

BIKE – Harlot

BIND – Unpleasant

BOOMERANG – Early return to base in trouble

BOOST – Manifold pressure

BREAK CLOUD – Decent below cloud base

BUMPY – Air turbulence

BURTON – Killed

C/B – Cloudbase

CARRIER – Aircraft carrier

CCS – Coastal Command Station

CFI – Chief flying instructor

CHEESED – Annoyed

CHOP – Killed

CHUTE – Parachute

CIRCUIT – Track around airfield before landing

CLAMP – Fog to ground level

CLAPPERS – Fast

CLOUD BORING – Decent through cloud above unknown ground height

CLUED UP – Informed

CLUSTER – A pack of incendiary bombs

CMC – Crew Movement Checkout

CONED – Held by searchlight beams

COOKIE – 4000 lb blockbuster bomb

CORKSCREW – Avoiding action

CRATE – Aircraft

CROW – Prostitute

DAFT – Bad

DECK – Ground

DELAY – Bomb with delay fuse

DFC – Distinguished Flying Cross

DFM – Distinguished Flying Medal

DICEY – Chancy

DIM VIEW – Angry

DISPERSAL – Parking bay

DITCH – Forced landing in the sea

DONK – Engine

DOODLEBUG – V1 Flying bomb

DOSE – Venereal Disease

DR – Dead reckoning

DRAK – Poor

DREM – Landing system

DRIFT – Sideways travel on landing approach

DRINK – Sea

DRONGO – Fool

DSO – Distinguished Service Order

ED – Embarkation Depot

ELSAN – Portable W.C.

ERK – Ground crew

ETA – Estimated time of arrival

FAA – Fleet Air Arm

FAN – Propeller

FEATHER – To rotate propeller blades with engine failure

FIDO – Fog dispersal airfield

FLAK – Antiaircraft fire

FLAP – Confusion or part of wings lowered for landing

FTHQ – Fighter Training Headquarters

FUNNELS – Final approach turning point

G/C – Group Captain

GAF – German Air Force

GAGGLE – Bomber Stream

GARDENING – Minelaying

GATE – Full throttle opening

GEN – Information

GEORGE – Automatic pilot

GLYCOL – Engine coolant

GONG – Decoration

GPI – Glide path indicator

GREASER – Ultra-smooth landing

GREMLIN – Unidentified trouble

GRILLED NAG – Horse steak

GROUPER – Group Captain

GUILD – Group of RAAF pilots

H-HOUR – Bombing time

HCU – Heavy Conversion Unit

HANG UPS – Unreleased bombs

HE – High explosive

HLB – High Level Bombing

HOLD OFF – Final landing correction

HOLYMAN – Padre

I/C – Intercom

I/F – Instrument flying

IFF – Identification friend or foe

INTRUDER – Nightime raider

JAM – Block transmission

JERRY – German force

L/I – Low-level Identification

LA – Land Army

LACW – Leading Aircraft Woman

LFS – Lancaster Finishing School

LIMIES – British, derogatory

M/B – Motorboat

M/O – Medical Officer

MEAT WAGON – Ambulance

MILK RUN – The usual flight path taken to Europe. In our case from Base, over Reading then out to sea from Bill of Portland

MOAN – Complaint

MOSSIE – Mosquito

N/F – Night Flying

NAAFI – Canteen

NAV – Navigator

NFT – Night Flight Test

NICKLE RAID – Flight to drop propaganda material over enemy territory.

OC – Officer Commanding

OCTANE – Petrol value

ORBIT – Circle

OTU – Operational training unit

OVERSHOOT – Approach too high

P/O – Pilot Officer

PANCAKE – Landing

PERIMETER – Outer taxiway

PERK – Vomit

PFF – Pathfinder force

PICKLE FACTORY – Buckingham Palace

PITCH – Propeller-blade angle

PLUTO – Pipeline under the ocean

PONGO – English

PORT – Left

POWDER ICE – Dry ice

PRANG – Crash or bombing

PREDICTED – Radar directed

PUCKER – Correct

PUNDIT – Red ground night marker

PYFO – Pull Your Finger Out

QBB – Cloud base

R/T – Radio telephone

RECCE – Reconnaissance

RED VEREY – Distress

REVS – Engine revolutions

RIME ICE – Hard ice

ROCKET – V2 Flying bomb

ROPEY – Bad

s/c – set course

S/L – Searchlight

S/L – Squadron Leader

SANDRA LIGHTS – Emergency orange lights

SAP – Sharp Armour Piercing

SBA – Standard Beam Approach

SCARECROW – Imitation burning aircraft

SCRAMBLE – Take off

SCRUBBED – Cancelled

SI – Starter ignition

SORT – Girl

SMOKEY JOE – Radio Position Fix

SP – Service police

SPAM – Canned spiced ham

SPERRY PANEL – Essential instrument panel

SPIT – Spitfire

SPLITOIT – Tight

SQUIRT – Jet aircraft

st cu – strato-cumulus cloud

STALL – Aircraft weight exceeds lift

STARBOARD – Right

STATIC FLAME – Electric charge

STOOGE – Second Pilot

SWP – South West Pacific

T/O – Take off

TC – Training Command

TALLY HO – Controller's OK to bomb target

TANNOY – Address system

THOU – Thousand

THREEPOINT – Perfect landing

TI – Target Indicator

TOTA – Take-off time allowed

TP – Turning point

TRIM – Lateral and longitudinal adjustment

TWITCH – Nervous shake of some sort

U/S – Unserviceable

UNDERCART – Undercarriage

UNDERSHOOT – Approach too low

VECTOR – Course

VEGETABLES – Mines

VEREY YY – Yellow flare

VHF – Very high frequency

W/C – Wing Commander

WAAF – Womens Auxiliary Air Force

WAKEY WAKEY – Anti-sleeping pill

WEAVE – Constant change of height, course and speed

WHEEL ON – Main wheels only landing

WIMPS – Wellingtons

WINDOW – Metallized strips to jam enemy radar

WIZARD – Good

WOP – Wireless operator

WODDA – Person

YANK – American

INDEX